Beyond Reading and Writing

WLU Series

Whole Language Umbrella

The Whole Language Umbrella, an organization within the National Council of Teachers of English, is composed of language arts educators and others who view whole language as a dynamic philosophy of education. Through this series, WLU encourages discussion of critical issues within whole language, including promoting research and study of and disseminating information of whole language and facilitating collaboration among teachers, researchers, parents, administrators, and teacher educators.

Series Co-editors: David E. Freeman, Fresno Pacific College, and Yvonne S. Freeman, Fresno Pacific College

Beyond Reading and Writing

Inquiry, Curriculum, and Multiple Ways of Knowing

Beth Berghoff
Indiana University

Kathryn A. Egawa
National Council of Teachers of English

Jerome C. Harste
Indiana University

Barry T. Hoonan
Bainbridge Island, Washington, School District

Whole Language Umbrella

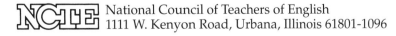
National Council of Teachers of English
1111 W. Kenyon Road, Urbana, Illinois 61801-1096

NCTE Editorial Board: Jacqueline Bryant, Kermit Campbell, Gail Wood, Xin Liu Gale, Sarah Hudelson, Jackie Swensson, Gerald R. Oglan, Helen Poole, Karen Smith, Chair, ex officio, Peter Feely, ex officio

Prepress Services: Electronic Imaging

Staff Editor: Rita D. Disroe

Interior Design: Doug Burnett

Cover Design: Pat Mayer

Front cover photographs by Photodisc.

Back cover photograph courtesy of Kathryn A. Egawa.

NCTE Stock Number: 23414-3050

Library of Congress Cataloging-in-Publication Data

Beyond reading and writing: inquiry, curriculum, and multiple ways of knowing/Beth Berghoff . . . [et al.].
    p. cm.
   Includes bibliographical references (p.).
   ISBN 0-8141-2341-4
   1. Language arts (Elementary). 2. Language experience approach in education. 3. Multiple intelligences. 4. Cognitive styles. 5. Critical pedagogy. I. Berghoff, Beth.

LB1576.B492 2000
372.6—dc21

                                                  99-087800

Contents

Introduction

In the story of the tortoise and the hare, the hare is much faster than the tortoise, yet through slow, deliberate action, the tortoise gets the job done. In many ways, this is a "tortoise" book. It has taken so long to get to publication that it actually provides a historical perspective. This book describes classroom teaching and teacher inquiry we conducted in the early 1990s, hardly cutting-edge practice as we near the year 2000—yet important nevertheless because it also explains what we learned through these experiences and why we think differently today. Therein lies the significance of the book. It documents a particular set of inquiries conducted by a particular whole language thought collective and provides insight into how we reconceptualized learning and curriculum as a result of our collaboration.

At the outset of our inquiries, we wondered how learning in our classrooms would change were we to expand our notions of literacy to include multiple sign systems and use inquiry as our framework for creating curriculum. With these questions in mind, we set about creating experiences to arrive at the answers. In this book, we articulate what we learned, both as means of gaining clarity for ourselves and as a means of sharing with others interested in the ideas of inquiry and multiple ways of knowing.

Our personal choices and connections led to this inquiry. Kathy Egawa and Beth Berghoff, both veteran elementary teachers, left their classrooms in 1989 to study with Jerry Harste and Carolyn Burke at Indiana University. Kathy and Beth were fascinated by the possibilities they only half understood when they read the book *Creating Classrooms for Authors* (1988), which Jerry and Carolyn authored with Kathy Short, who is now a professor at the University of Arizona. Under Carolyn and Jerry's guidance, Kathy and Beth explored the socio-psycholinguistic and semiotic theories of meaning making, and they began to see the value of a curriculum built around inquiry and multiple ways of knowing. This discovery led them to return to elementary classrooms to put theory into practice, each working with a collaborative teacher in her own context. Kathy worked with fifth- and sixth-grade teacher Barry Hoonan in Washington, and Beth, with first-grade teacher Susan Hamilton in Indiana. Meanwhile, Jerry continued to fine-tune the theory and explore it with other educators in a variety of contexts.

In 1994, the authors of this book—Kathy, Barry, Jerry, and Beth—presented a session about the theory and our classroom inquiries at the NCTE Annual Convention. (Susan stayed home with her new baby.) And in 1995, the group collaborated again, conducting a workshop about inquiry and multiple ways of knowing for NCTE Annual Convention participants. This book is an outgrowth of those presentations and the ongoing conversations. At times, the story in this book is told in one voice. At other times, it is told in a collective "we" voice that represents this collaborative group.

For us, the notion of a curriculum based on inquiry and multiple ways of knowing has become a complex and powerful concept. In practice, this model fundamentally changes what we do in classrooms. And we believe it is what Simon (1992) calls a "project of possibility"—educational practice whose fundamental purpose is to expand what it means to be human and to contribute to the establishment of a just and compassionate community. Theorizing about these two elements of curriculum, inquiry and multiple ways of knowing, has given us a new perspective that puts the learner rather than standards or disciplines at the center of curriculum. We appreciate the complexity of coming to know and the absurdity of operating as if curriculum could deliver standardized results. We are currently working on adding a third dimension to our model of curriculum, the dimension of critical literacy. As we make it possible for learners to be more in control of their inquiries and to make more choices about how to think and communicate, we are learning that our classrooms are microcosms of the larger society. And we recognize that we have a responsibility to reculture our learning communities so that the learners experience and understand equality and justice. As Schor (1990) puts it, "if we do not teach in opposition to the existing inequality of races, classes, and sexes, then we are teaching to support it. If we don't teach critically against domination in society, then we allow dominant forces a free hand in school and out" (p. 347).

Readers will not find much about this third dimension of curriculum in this book because that focus evolved as a result of the work described in this book. For our thought collective, developing an understanding of inquiry and multiple ways of knowing came first and then set the stage for this new generation of critical conversations. Consequently, this book does not address the critical aspects of curriculum. Rather, it focuses throughout on the notions of inquiry and multiple ways of knowing.

Over the years, the whole language community has expanded concepts by looking for the larger patterns in learning and living. In 1988, it was revolutionary to think of "literacy" as more than reading and writing, yet the whole language community was thinking of literacy as the ability to communicate successfully in all variety of contexts and for many purposes. And today, Sumara (1996) asserts that we should not think of school as a place where we create readers, but rather as a place where students learn to live lives that include reading. *Curriculum* is another word that has taken on drastically different meaning over time. The whole language community has morphed it from a word that describes the written scope and sequence of expected learning to a word that means a co-constructed learning process, the shared life of students and teachers in classrooms.

Inquiry, like *literacy* and *curriculum,* has multifaceted meaning. On one level, *inquiry* means learning driven by the learner's personal question or questions. There are always questions. Our lives are full of ambiguity, and we have to continually ask "What does this mean?" or "What do I need to know about that?" Our questions originate from what we already know, and we pursue them by making predictions, examining assumptions, gathering more information, and seeking alternative perspectives and new possibilities. In essence, inquiry is learning.

On another level, inquiry is a way of knowing, a willingness to undergo a journey, to tolerate ambiguity, to sort through multiple perspectives, and to trust abduction—those leaps of insights that totally restructure what is known. Those who assume a questioning stance depend on conversations with others and understand that they must give back something of themselves in return. Inquirers expect to be changed by their work and to take new action based on what they learn.

We also use the word *inquiry* to refer to the social process of collaborative inquiry. In *Creating Classrooms for Authors and Inquirers,* Short, Harste, and Burke (1996) describe the underlying processes that support learning communities in pursuing their interests and questions collaboratively. In an inquiry cycle, members of a learning community make personal connections and observations; they collaborate with others to experiment, discuss, transmediate, attend to anomalies, present information, and reflect. In the end, these learners take action in response to their new understandings. Teachers nudge learners along in this constructive process by providing key experiences and time for reading, writing, talking, and transmediating. Learners are helped to clarify their ideas and to create artifacts, to make choices and to have a voice in a variety of groups.

Collaborative inquiry depends on a learning community's ability to work democratically. It requires respect for and the positive use of diversity, and learners are expected to arrive at understandings, rather than at answers. Understandings, according to Carolyn

Burke, last only until learners have time to ask new questions or to create more compelling theories.

> We don't inquire to eliminate alternatives but to find more functional understandings—to create diversity, broaden our thinking, and ask more complex questions. We can end up *more* confused, not less confused, but our confusion reflects new questions that are more complex and based on deeper insights. (Short et al., 1996, p. 9)

"Sign systems," another term that may be unfamiliar to many readers, comes from the discipline of semiotics, the study of meaning (Solomon, 1988). Sign systems—such as art, music, drama, mathematics, and language—are communication systems. We use them to construct and express meaning. These systems resemble language in that each sign system is comprised of forms of representation and conventions. Each sign system is also uniquely different from language. Drawing or painting, for example, uses the elements of color, shape, and line in a simultaneous presentation. When viewing a picture, the learner is presented with all the information at once. In the case of a song or story, the learner is presented with signs arrayed across time. There is a linear quality to the media. Music can express feelings we cannot put into words; language is a better medium for humor than math; and math can represent concepts not easily represented in art, and so on.

We use sign systems in coordinated ways. We draw maps to explain our verbal directions; authors and illustrators work toward a marriage of art and words; and spoken language is supplemented by gestures, postures, glances, grimaces, shrugs, and grunts. Songs and movies incorporate language with music and scenes. We experience sign systems in many combinations, because they are complementary systems and our thought is a rich dialogue of these many sign systems. They allow us to know and express what we know in multiple ways (Berghoff, 1993).

Semioticians assert that a *sign*, the basic unit of meaning common to all sign systems, can be anything that stands to someone for something. They point out that a sign does not transmit meaning. In other words, seeing or hearing a sign does not ensure that a meaning will spring into one's mind. For example, the reader might run across the word *chien*. Does the notion of dog spring up into the reader's consciousness? Probably only if the reader speaks French, for *chien* is the French word for *dog*.

Signs mediate, or stand between, two human meaning makers. Signs are perceptible forms we use to express or construct meanings. There is not a strict one-to-one relationship between the meaning expressed by the originator of a sign and the meaning constructed by the person perceiving the sign. The person who perceives the sign attributes meaning to the sign based on his or her personal knowledge. Slippage does occur in this process of mediated exchange, for none of us can draw from exactly the same set of personal experiences. Fortunately, though, we think more alike than not, and our constructed meanings are usually quite similar or parallel to the meanings expressed. This results from signs becoming associated with particular meanings as we use them with others and with ourselves to communicate and live our lives. The word *chien* will evoke meaning only if the individual has previous experience with the sign. The more familiar English word *dog* may trigger a complex meaning, one complete with emotions of fear or affinity for dogs and the concept of *dog* that has developed within the culture. Through our use of signs, we share common belief systems and conceptual views of the world with those around us.

Sign systems are the psychological tools that allow humans to think, communicate, and learn. Vygotsky (1978) explains that they give us the power to reflect on behavior and experiences. Signs augment the human ability to remember and construct meaning. We can make a note to remind ourselves to do something, we can read about what's happening in our community, or we can participate in specialized knowledge communities—all through the use of signs. We develop cognitively by using signs to inform ourselves and to interact with others. Manipulating signs within a social context allows us to develop higher-order thinking, that is, logical memory, selective attention, decision making, and language comprehension (Dixson-Krauss, 1996).

As meaning makers, we rely on the sign systems we know best. The more experience we have with a sign system, the more likely we are to choose it to represent our thinking, and the more aware we are of its presence in our environment.

Kathy Short (1990) has been working with multiple sign systems in curriculum for several years. In an early classroom study, Short set up a learning environment in a third-grade classroom that immersed students in learning about and using sign systems. The students spent a month exploring literature and tools from various sign systems. In their discussions, they talked about how one system differed from another and how they felt about using particular systems. The tools of each sign system became part of the classroom environment and the children used them in creating literature response projects.

In interviews and reflections, the children in this third grade indicated that the experience of using multiple sign systems changed what they attended to. After the study, one child said, "I look at the world differently. It's like a big dance. People look like they are dancing to me, not just walking." Another child said, "I hear music when I read."

The children in this study acknowledged that different sign systems had different potentials for conveying their messages and that they could integrate sign systems to more effectively share what they wanted others to know. They were reiterating what Elliot Eisner (1982) has been saying to educators for nearly two decades, "The [sign systems] we use to construe the world not only guide our attention to it, but when used to represent it, both constrain and make possible, what we are able to convey" (p. 7). Eisner warns that we should not be satisfied with curriculum that focuses only on language and mathematics. In accepting such, we relinquish too much our potential for knowing the world. Our curricula need to value all sign systems.

There is yet another warning in Eisner's statement. He reminds us that when we borrow signs from sign systems to communicate and think, we also borrow cultural ways of thinking. This may seem a trivial matter, but it is not always so. Solomon (1988), for example, discusses the meaning of high-heeled shoes. He says, "To women who wear them, they may be merely fashionable articles of dress, but to feminist decoders the shoes signify the desire of male-dominated culture to disable women physically, to keep them jacked up on heels that prevent them from running away" (p. 17). He points out that there are always multiple ways to interpret signs and that we must be critical users who interrogate the ideology behind our signs. When we lack critical thought, we often unknowingly perpetuate cultural practices we ourselves do not consciously endorse.

When we started the inquiry underlying this book, we believed that sign systems made up the central element of multiple ways of knowing, and we devoted our energy to expanding our knowledge about and use of sign systems in teaching and learning. In retrospect, however, we see that although sign systems make up an important part of multiple ways of knowing, they are but one of the many ways in which knowing is constructed differently from individual to individual. Learning is always impacted by social ways of knowing such as sign systems, disciplines, and discourse communities—as well as the individual learner's questions, interests, understandings, and perceptual strengths. We experienced significant changes in our students' learning when we incorporated a greater variety of sign systems into our curriculum, and we see this as one step teachers can make toward a curriculum that embraces multiple ways of knowing. It opens the door to a reconceptualization of learners' development and of our role as teachers.

"Multiple ways of knowing," as we use the term in this book, is a shift from a constructivist perspective to a semiotic one. We believe learners who are making meaning draw simultaneously on different dimensions of knowing—different forms of expression (sign systems), different kinds of ideas (knowledge systems), and different cultural frameworks (sociocultural systems). These different ways of knowing are both the source of and the result of our diversity. And the broader the spectrum of ways of knowing a learner can access, the richer the learning.

When we presented at the 1994 NCTE Annual Convention, Jerry opened the session by explaining why inquiry and multiple ways of knowing should be central to literacy and learning. He reconstructs his presentation in Chapter 1, where he offers six points of departure for changing practice in schools and illustrates each of these with drawings, artifacts, and personal stories. The next three chapters are theory-into-practice chapters. In Chapter 2, Beth describes her work with Susan to create inquiry and develop curriculum introducing multiple ways of knowing in a first-grade classroom. This chapter provides insight into how such a curriculum actually worked on a day-to-day basis and how the children learned. In Chapters 3 and 4, Kathy and Barry tell their stories of seeing children in new dimensions. As they personally developed more complex understandings of inquiry and multiple ways of knowing, they began to see more of both in their students' learning. Kathy focuses on how this new insight helped her support and understand the learning of Scott (second grade), while Barry focuses on Nathaniel (fifth grade). Both boys were struggling with traditional aspects of literacy. Language was not their strong suit; consequently, they were doing poorly with reading and writing tasks and appeared to be unmotivated and significantly less capable than their peers. Kathy and Barry learned to suspend this limiting view of the boys and to look for larger patterns in their learning.

The last chapter in the book presents some of the insights we have gained by undertaking this inquiry. We note that certain students look stronger when we provide more choices of ways to express themselves and more support for prolonged engagement with their own questions. As teachers, we can learn to "read" a child from multiple perspectives and to open ourselves to those moments that totally restructure our sense of who the child is and how he or she learns. This depends on continually asking our own questions about the learners: How does learning work for this child? In this social context? In this sign system? In other sign systems? With this question as opposed to other questions?

We also explore what we have discovered in our attempts to expand our understanding and comfort level with different sign systems. Each of us has made a commitment to push beyond what we are comfortable doing with sign systems and to expand our personal repertoires of experiences as well as our abilities to integrate more sign systems into our teaching. We believe that one of the ways we can disrupt the text of school is to stop doing school the ways we always have done and to start doing it in more artful ways, to think of literacy as something that develops across sign systems, not just in language.

Finally, we expand on what we have learned from conducting inquiry both personally and in the classroom. Inquiry, unlike rote learning, depends on lived experience. It depends on those with whom we learn and on the resources we can access. It depends on our internal schemas and our understandings of the underlying processes that contribute to developing larger chunks of meaning. Inquiry requires us to muck around, to reflect on our own learning, to challenge each others' thinking, to theorize, to present, and to be social learners in countless other ways. Inquiry is about the relationships and rhythms of learning, about ways of knowing that cannot be easily expressed in language, and can be best understood through experience.

We are excited by the ways in which our teaching has changed as a result of this shared inquiry. We try to immerse learners in contexts rich in multiple ways of knowing and to invite their inquiry and collaboration. We hope this book helps other teachers think about curriculum in new ways, too. Schools can be very constructive places when we appreciate all aspects of the learning process. Learners can develop wide-ranging sensibilities that enable them to think and communicate in complex ways, to make sense of multiple perspectives, to continually revise their personal identities and theories of the world, and to positively shape their lives and communities . . . if we as educators make it possible.

Six Points of Departure

Jerome C. Harste

How we envision literacy makes a difference. If we see it as meaning making and not meaning making plus inquiry, we fail to envision all that literacy might be. If we see literacy as language and not language plus other sign systems, we also fail to envision all that literacy might be. This lack of vision is obvious in our schools. We have barely scratched the surface of what there is to know about the complexity of literacy and learning.

Currently talk about school restructuring abounds. Unfortunately, however, much of this talk deals only with surface changes to the nature of classrooms. Instead of one grade level, schools are moving to multiage classrooms. Instead of moving children to a new teacher each year, schools are experimenting with multiyear classrooms. While reforms of this sort are long overdue, they in themselves do not constitute real change in education.

If interaction patterns in classrooms don't change, then nothing is really different. One can have multiage and multiyear classrooms and nevertheless have dreadful instruction. To change education requires a shift in the nature of teacher-student, student-student, and student-content area interaction. None of this is simple.

For example, we have been exploring the notion of transmediation, that is, taking what you know in one sign system and recasting it in another (Suhor, 1992), by using an instructional strategy called Sketch to Stretch developed several years ago (Harste, Short & Burke, 1988). This strategy asks readers to draw a sketch "symbolizing what this story means to you." Sketches are shared through another strategy called Save the Last Word for the Artist (Harste, Short & Burke, 1988, 1995) in which the artist holds up his or her picture, everyone in the group guesses what the artist has tried to portray and, as a way to end, the artist gets the last word. When used together, these two strategies are extremely generative. My students and I are always amazed at the new insights we get into old stories as a result of participating in Sketch to Stretch and Save the Last Word for the Artist.

Several teacher-researchers have used Sketch to Stretch as the basis of their educational inquiries. Marjorie Siegel (1984) explored "reading as signification" by using these strategies with a fourth-grade class of students. Interestingly, because she pulled children from the classroom to do Sketch to Stretch with them, they came to perceive it as "fun," but not part of "real reading." That was the stuff that went on under the direction of the classroom teacher. Phyllis Whitin (1996) used Sketch to Stretch as the basic organizational device for her seventh-grade reading program. Each evening students would draw a sketch of what the story meant to them and then use this sketch to begin a new round of classroom conversations. Over the course of the year, Phyllis varied the strategy's format by asking students to identify pieces of existing art they thought personified stories they had read and, on still other occasions, she asked students to represent the stories they had read "mathematically" by using pie graphs and the like. The tale of her work is told in a book entitled *Sketching Stories, Stretching Minds* (1996) and documents the significant growth students made in her class relative to reading.

I've also seen Sketch to Stretch used much less effectively. Many teachers (even those who experience the strategy firsthand under my guidance!) will go back to their classrooms and modify the directions, asking students to draw "a favorite part of the story" rather than "symbolize what the story means to you." This simple change alters the strategy completely. It calls for representation rather than metaphorical thinking. This is like asking a literal question instead of a question that encourages critical thinking.

As defined earlier, to take what you know in one sign system (language) and recast it in another (art) is a process called transmediation. While talk mediates experience, taking what you talked about and drawing a sketch "transmediates" it. Sketch to Stretch was designed to encourage transmediation. The meaning readers make becomes a metaphor that also needs to be read. Readers read the sketch as a metaphorical statement about a bigger process, typically some truth about how they see the world working. Sketch to Stretch supports the process of projection. Literacy is not only comprehending but also using what was understood to understand the unfamiliar. Other participants, of course, complicate as well as enliven the discussion. Their projections differ, often creating new tensions as well as new possibilities.

Recognizing the subtle difference between sketching a favorite part of the story and sketching what the story means depends on understanding theoretically what happens in each case. When a child draws a scene from the story, who can argue with his or her representation? Even if such pictures are shared to create conversation, the conversation is focused inward (on the picture and the scene it represents) rather than outward (on the metaphorical meaning of the sketch). The conversation will be a retelling of the story rather than an expansion of its meaning to other aspects of life.

Transmediation is one concept that has significantly changed our thinking. Transmediation is an instance of metaphor, yet more. To create a metaphor, the language user searches for an equivalent to the experience, often one that is more familiar and that puts an experience in a new light. Transmediation pushes beyond metaphor by taking what is known in one sign system and recasting it in another. Because each sign system is unique and best suited to a particular perspective of the world, there are often no direct equivalencies. It is difficult to express horror in mathematical symbols, and "love" is expressed quite differently in art than in language. Moving from sign system to sign system is like turning an artifact so that we suddenly see a new facet that was previously hidden from our view.

We have learned that transmediation is most powerful in a social setting. Sketches need the interpretation of others to fulfill their promise. The process is designed to disrupt the existing text, to open it up anew. The person who drew the sketch often gains new insights from hearing what others have to say.

Majorie Siegel (1995) argues that transmediation represents the core of literacy. Learners take what they know and symbolize it. To be meaningful, they draw on their knowledge of sign systems, for these systems represent social agreements about signs and meaning. In sharing, the learners come to understand that all meaning is negotiated and that the meaning attributed to signs depends on the context and social interaction. These literacy processes are what Sketch to Stretch is all about.

This discussion of transmediation reflects just one example of the kind of conversations I would like to start. I strongly believe that a holistic, inquiry-based curriculum, at the foundation of which rests multiple ways of knowing, has the potential to revolutionize schools. Therefore, I think we must envision and create curriculum that places inquiry and sign systems—art, music, dance, drama, and movement—at the center of the learning process, rather than in the peripheral position of curricular frills, mere respites one ventures into by way of taking a break from the hard work of learning language and mathematics. What we are learning is exciting, because it does disrupt the existing text. We have experienced how such a curriculum makes new perspectives possible, helps us to see the strengths of previously marginalized learners, changes us personally, and enhances the humane and critical aspects of literacy and learning.

What I wish to do in this chapter is set forth some points of departure. I would like to move beyond cute activities and seriously explore sign systems as central to the learning process, for sign systems create tension, offer new perspectives, and set in motion the twin processes of reflection and reflexivity.

Point of Departure #1

The goal of a good language arts program is to expand communication potential.

Often we hear children at about the third-grade level say they can't sing. By fourth grade many children say they can't draw, and dancing with their classmates is something they've long ago rejected. This concerns me, and I hope it concerns you, too. Young children love to move, to sing, to draw. What has happened, then?

It seems obvious that in our teaching of art, music, and movement, we've convinced children they are not capable. As children progress through school, they become more and more dependent on language as their primary means of communication. Unfortunately, most language arts curricula inadvertently contribute to this problem—perhaps because the importance of these other sign systems is not recognized or because they are trivialized in the translation to classroom practice. Teachers often think art is easy, whereas language is tough. Pictures are concrete; language, abstract. Art is optional; language, mandatory. "Write a story, and then, if time remains, you might like to illustrate it."

Carolyn Burke (1991) drew the sketch in Figure 1 to illustrate two important points. First, every sign system contributes something unique to the making and sharing of meaning. When we limit ourselves to language, we cut ourselves off from other ways of knowing. As Elliot Eisner would say, our point of experience is so narrow that we don't even recognize what we don't know. A good language arts program should open up, rather than close down, our communicative options. A language arts program that emphasizes language at the expense of art and other sign systems fails to serve anyone well. Children whose strength is not language are denied access. Children whose strength is language are not given opportunities to extend their knowing and thereby develop new ways to communicate with themselves and others.

Second, Figure 1 suggests that every instance of making and sharing meaning is a multimodal event involving many sign systems in addition to language. As an example, watch two people in conversation. They use posture, gesture, facial expressions, intonation, laughter, and even silence, to get their message across. Picture storybooks may be viewed as language, but in reality, the pictures carry as much of the message as do the words on the page. McDonald's uses its name, as well as its golden arches, to produce readers. Just ask parents of a three-year-old. They often drive miles out of their way to avoid driving by a fast-food restaurant. Even college textbooks use illustrations and sketches to present their ideas and make them comprehensible. Speakers use overhead projectors, drama, and concrete examples to drive points home.

Figure 1.
Multiple Ways of Knowing
(adapted from Short, Harste
& Burke, 1996)

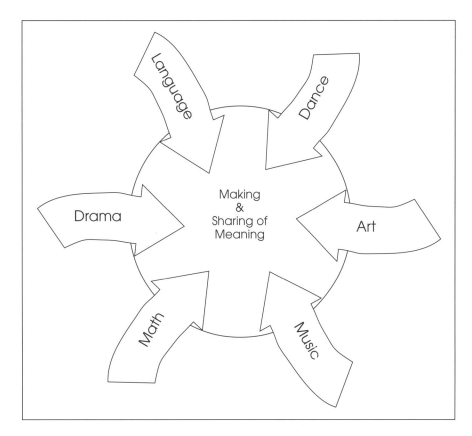

In his 1996 book, *Changing Our Minds*, Miles Myers argues that, as a society, we are doing exactly what the title of his book suggests—changing our minds about literacy. Given technological changes in our society and advances in the field of research, reader response and authorship no longer constitute what it means to be literate. Citizens of the twenty-first century will need to know how to read, as well as how to create, multivocal and multimodal texts. By multivocal, Myers means texts that respect and reflect multiple voices. By multimodal, he means texts that use images—as well as sounds, music, movement, and language—to communicate their messages. People creating homepages for the Internet are already involved in this kind of work.

English/language arts teachers are once again under the gun. Now we are being asked to prepare children for a literate future we ourselves have only just begun to grasp. Yet this does not mean that what we have done in the past is wrong, only that it fails to measure up today. In order to prepare children who can read and create such texts, we need to conceptualize literacy and literacy education very

Figure 2.
Alison, Age Six:
Uninterrupted Writing

differently. I believe that seeing sign systems as central to learning is a first step in that process.

Point of Departure #2

Taking what we know in one sign system and recasting it in terms of another is both natural and basic to literacy.

At six years of age, Alison had a telephone conversation with her friend Jennifer (Harste, Woodward & Burke, 1984). They decided to meet after church on Sunday and play ballerina. Alison would get her leotard, slippers, and hair ribbons from her dresser, and Jennifer would bring her leotard, slippers, and hair ribbons with her in a bag. When Alison got off the phone, she went to her room and recorded her conversation. To do so, she used math, art, and language, as shown in Figure 2.

Alison forced us to rethink literacy. She showed us that literacy is much broader than language. When literacy is defined as the processes by which we, as humans, mediate the world for the purpose of learning, then this language story demonstrates that Alison is engaged in the stuff of "real" literacy. To mediate the world is to create sign systems—mathematics, art, music, dance, language—that stand between the world as it is and the world as we perceive it. These sign systems act as lenses that permit us to better understand ourselves and our world.

Alison's final product is an elegant summarization of a complex literacy event. How many of us wish we could take paper and pencil and so easily portray an experience? No one taught Alison to do this. In the course of living in a multimodal world, she figured out how sign systems work in the service of her needs, wants, and desires.

Teachers often view transmediation—the use and movement among sign systems that Alison has done so readily here—as an instructional strategy rather than as part and parcel of every act of literacy inside and outside school. All cultures have devised multiple ways to mean. Further, the ability to make sense by moving between and among sign systems begins early and develops to sophisticated levels (Harste, Woodward & Burke, 1984).

Lessons such as this one are important for all of us to make firsthand. They teach us to trust children and the learning process. What goes wrong in many schools stems from a failure to understand literacy in all its complexity and thereby prevents our trusting learners and the learning process. Further, failing to understand literacy as a multimodal event results in restrictions and reduces options for the learner. By being able to move to alternate sign systems, children can "wiggle" the system to have it make more personal sense to them (Ericksen, 1985). By underestimating learners and the learning process, we often restrict learners by simplifying tasks—thereby decreasing opportunities to keep conversation dialogical and learning generative.

Point of Departure #3

Just as reading involves the flexible use of all cue systems, so also literacy entails the flexible use of all sign systems in the creation of a successful text given a specific context.

In 1967, Kenneth Goodman did a very simple thing that revolutionized the teaching of reading. Instead of building a model of the reading process based on adult logic, he handed readers a book, asked them to read, and then tape-recorded their readings. Based on his observations and analysis of their reading, he devised a psycholinguistic model of the reading process (Goodman, 1967).

Goodman defined a miscue as the difference between an expected and an observed response during reading. Figure 3 shows a miscue. In this case the reader, John, has read a section of the story as "John opened the door. There were amazing . . . magnifying . . . magazines and boxes of clothes."

The little *c* in the circle means that the reader corrected the miscue. What is significant about this miscue is that given the letters in *magazine*—M, A, G, A, Z, I, N, E—the reader came up with two words, within the period of about two seconds—amazing and magnifying—with many of the same letters. This feat, repeated again and again as people read, gives us pause. The mind is a truly marvelous thing. Although we have difficulty explaining the rapidity of the miscues, we know that letter-sound or graphophonemic information was involved in the production of the miscue.

Figure 3.
John: Miscue Sample

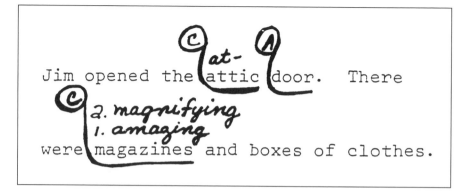

Notice that the reader adds *-ing* to the ending of each miscue. The helping verb *were* sets up the expectation that an *-ing* word will follow. Here's proof that the reader is using syntax, the structure of language, to make predictions while reading. Proficient readers unconsciously ask themselves, "Does what I read sound like language to me?" If it doesn't, they self-correct based on their intuitive sense of the grammatical rules that govern word order and the flow of language.

Another thing to notice is that the reader corrects his miscue. Obviously, *were magnifying and* doesn't make sense. The reader goes back, resamples from the text and aligns what is being said with what is on the page. Proficient readers also continually ask themselves, "Does what I read make sense to me?" In this case, the linguistic system that triggered the rereading is called semantics, or meaning.

All three systems of language—graphophonemic, syntax, and semantics—work together when we read. The discovery that the subsystems of language work together in reading led to a revolution in reading instruction. Therefore, teachers today give children with whom they work entire texts to read rather than lists of words. When word lists are used, readers cannot rely on their knowledge of syntax and semantics to predict or self-correct. They are forced to depend on the graphophonemic system alone to acquire the information they need. Deprived of all the language cues typically available in the real world, students find that reading in school often becomes harder than it is in real life.

As a result of Kenneth Goodman's work, we now understand that readers make use of three cuing systems as they read. The difference between proficient readers and less proficient readers lies in the flexibility displayed in the use of the three systems. Less proficient readers use all three systems on occasion but tend to overuse one system at the expense of the others.

Figure 4.
Emily, Kindergarten:
Uninterrupted Writing

Now, I would like to do for literacy what Kenneth Goodman did for reading. I would like to argue that literacy necessitates the flexible use of sign systems to create a successful text given a specific context.

My absolute favorite example of a very effective, as well as multimodal, text is from Emily, age five. She writes, "Once I get into books, I can't get out." As shown in Figure 4, her drawing of herself in the book does more than replicate what she means, as without it, her text would not have nearly the impact it now does.

This text illustrates the point. It consists of language as well as figures and artifacts. To be literate, one must take what one knows and create, in light of the audience and the context in which one is working, a successful text. For example, were I talking to my mother about whole language, I would create a text very different from what I would create were I talking with teachers and even very different still were I talking to researchers. Each of these texts requires the orchestration of sign systems in very different ways. To be literate, I need to flexibly use a variety of sign systems.

Once children have researched topics of interest, they should be invited to make multiple presentations to different audiences,

audiences that require the presentations to be orchestrated in different ways. Persons who can communicate knowledge in only one way are not as literate as futurists such as Miles Myers (1996) suggest they will have to be.

Point of Departure #4

I cannot talk about sign systems except in relationship to education as inquiry.

Figure 5 shows how we are now envisioning curriculum. The core of curriculum is personal and social knowing. Curriculum begins in voice. Learners have the right, as well as the responsibility, to name and theorize their world. They also have the right and responsibility to interrogate their own naming, as well as the naming of others, but to say this is not to deny that curriculum begins with voice. It is the first step, yet must not stop there.

Subject areas now have a stranglehold on curriculum. Even "integrated curriculum" begins with the assumption that the subject areas are rightfully the center of the curriculum, and the only real problem is that we need to better integrate them. Instead of emphasizing the facts and skills of subject areas, we can focus on knowledge systems as perspectives that inquirers might take in exploring a topic of interest. Knowledge systems resemble syntax in language. Just as syntax provides an explanation of how language is structured, so, too, knowledge systems represent various perspectives or ways of structuring knowledge about the world. Each knowledge system has its own focusing questions. Historians are interested in how the past might inform the present and future. Ecologists are interested in how what we do affects the balance of nature. By rotating our questions through the knowledge systems, we gain new insights. In Figure 5, knowledge systems become research perspectives used by inquirers, rather than dead bodies of knowledge to be memorized and forgotten.

Language, art, music, drama, mathematics, and movement are sign systems. They represent ways humans have learned to mediate the world in an attempt to make and share meaning. Although the history of each of these sign systems is a discipline in itself, in their tool form they are the vehicles by which we code and encode our world. We can, for example, use any and all of these tools in talking about any subject we wish to talk about. They represent, in the truest sense, communication potential.

The wedge in Figure 5 represents inquiry. It cuts across all the other systems, thereby suggesting that an alternative way to organize curriculum is around the inquiry questions of learners. Knowledge systems and sign systems become perspectives and tools that inquirers flexibly use in collaboration with others to explore, share,

Figure 5.
Curriculum as Critical Inquiry
(adapted from Short, Harste
& Burke, 1996)

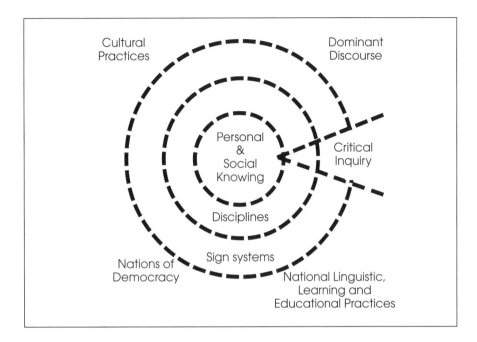

and make meaning. Figure 5 suggests that the smallest unit of curriculum is the focused inquiry.

It is important to understand that the meanings that get made, shared, and explored are determined in part by the context of situations in which education is embedded. Education in our society means education for a democracy. When some sign systems or ways of knowing are valued over others, inquiry is affected.

We are not suggesting that inquiry is innocent. Because of the nature of our society and the ways of knowing it's values, inquiry is also tied up in issues of access, equity, and justice. Not only are we challenged to understand the systems of meaning that operate in our society but we are challenged as well to interrogate the structures that keep those systems of meaning in place. Inquiry is, of course, the way to do this and hence why the sketch turns on itself by inviting learners to interrogate their old and new naming of the world.

Curriculum as inquiry is not something that happens from two o'clock to three o'clock in the afternoon in school. It is not a clever device for integrating the curriculum through themes. Nor is it a skill we can teach by doing a unit on the "scientific method" in science. Curriculum as inquiry is a philosophy, a way to view education holistically. Inquiry is education; education, inquiry.

To explore these ideas further, Jean Anne Clyde and I organized a graduate course between our two universities, the University of Kentucky and Indiana University. One of the course requirements was to create a series of curricular engagements that invited students to think in some sign system besides language. During one sharing time, Vicki Bumann and Darlene Horton shared an "inventor project" they had worked on in Vicki's classroom. While inventing is neither a sign system nor a particularly hot "social issue," they rationalized that inventing would support visual and mathematical thinking, as well as privilege some groups more than others. They began their inventing project by bringing in a guest inventor. His advice was that inventors identify recurring problems by thinking about their lives and checking with friends and family members for ideas. He suggested they assume other people had the same problems they did, focus on a problem that interested them, and then brainstorm with others about how they might solve it.

To support and help organize the children, Vicki and Darlene had prepared an *Inventors Notebook* in which the children could record information they collected and sketch possible inventions. Victor, a Chapter 1 student who participated in this experience, did everything the inventor suggested. He created a list of problems. He checked his list against what his teachers and parents thought were problems. He investigated to identify an inquiry topic.

Victor chose a very real, personal problem. He repeatedly lost his pencil, a situation that was driving him and his teachers "nuts" —to use his own take on the issue. Resolved to hold on to his pencil, Victor brainstormed ideas with members of his family and found a practical solution. Using two pieces of velcro, he wrapped one around the top of his pencil and stuck the other piece to his desk. At the time Vicki and Darlene were sharing the story, Victor had not lost his pencil in over a week!

Further, the teachers reported that several other children in the class decided they wanted Victor's invention. He sold his invention to others for twenty-five cents. Predictably, because of his success, other children began to see him as a marketing expert and consulted him about which inventions were worth making.

Victor had not been a very popular child in the class and was not a proficient user of written language. He had been perceived as an outsider. Yet within a week, he had begun to gain a new identity for himself.

I like this story. It moves the study of sign systems beyond cute and intuitive to focus on how sign systems affect what curriculum in a democratic society might be.

Point of Departure #5

Sign systems can be used to enhance all the underlying processes of literacy.

Figure 6.
Underlying Processes in
Inquiry (adapted from Short,
Harste & Burke, 1996)

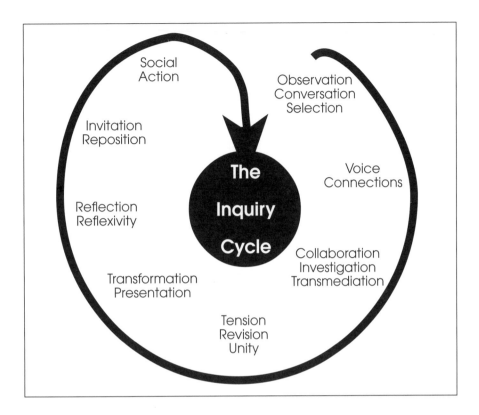

As we have explored curriculum as inquiry, one of the major questions to have emerged concerns the role of sign systems within inquiry. In our early work, we fell into the trap of studying sign systems separately from inquiry in much the same way in which schools had previously asked students to read and write without having a purpose that made sense to the students. When isolated and explored on their own, the functionality of the systems is lost.

Within the context of inquiry, however, sign systems serve an important role in expanding, understanding, and more fully appreciating ideas. In this context they are not just frills, but tools for gaining new perspectives on the world.

Figure 6 represents a sketch of the inquiry process based on what we currently know about the role that language plays in learning. It is a working sketch which assumes that other sign systems play a similar role. This assumption is significant for two reasons. First, the use of sign systems is most often relegated to the presentation phase of learning—"You might want to include some charts, graphs, or photographs in your report"—rather than used to help learners gain a new perspective or see the world differently. Figure 6 is meant to suggest that art can be used to acquire voice, observe the world more carefully, gain new perspectives, disrupt the typical way this topic has been thought about, identify qualities previously overlooked, make better presentations, reflect more thoughtfully, and contribute to a more well-rounded understanding and set of actions. Art, in this case, is being used metaphorically. Music, drama, mathematics, and movement can play similar functions.

The second assumption being made in this sketch is that sign systems operate "like language." This is a fairly dangerous assumption. Other sign systems do things that language does not do, or else they would cease to exist. We are language educators, so we know more about language than we do other systems. We have to be careful, then, that we do not let what we know mask what is possible. We have a lot to learn about the role of sign systems in learning. To think we already know what it is we need to know is to arrest the learning process. Despite this, the best hypothesis we can posit is that other sign systems are at least as powerful as language.

I recently saw a Reggio Emilia tape in which a group of four- and five-year-olds create "An Amusement Park for the Birds" (Forman & Gandini, 1994). In this videotape, and in *The Hundred Languages of Children* (Edwards, Gandini & Forman, 1993), preschoolers are constantly invited to use art to observe their world more closely. Given the details and lifelike portraits these five-year-olds produce by drawing, we need to interrogate the assumptions upon which we currently base educational decisions. Clearly, something is happening in programs that support multiple ways of knowing, such as Reggio Emilia, that has not been happening in our verbocentric curricula of the past.

Three aspects of the sketch in Figure 6 bear particular notice. First, the cycle calls attention to the underlying processes of inquiry. If this cycle is our framework for thinking about education, then curriculum should focus on and support the underlying processes of inquiry. Activities that are planned should do more than keep children busy. They need to lead somewhere. While they might highlight a particular process (help children build from the known, find their own inquiry questions, gain new perspectives, and so forth), they also need to fit a larger purpose.

Second, the cycle focuses on learning, or inquiry, which represents the larger purpose. Education, first and foremost, is about learning, about outgrowing ourselves through inquiry. Inquiry is not a technique, but rather, the very focus of education. In the past, we have taught problem solving as part of a unit in mathematics, and inquiry, as part of a unit in science or history, and then we were finished. As a curricular frame, Figure 6 puts inquiry at the center of what education is all about.

Third, Figure 6 is also meant as a sketch of professional education. Teaching itself is a matter of inquiry. Children serve as our
curricular informants and collaborators, but there is no getting
teaching right. As professionals we, too, are always learning and
growing.

The whole of education is one cloth. Theory and practice go
hand in hand. How we think about education affects what we do in
the name of education. Figure 6 is a theoretical hypothesis. That we,
and the teachers with whom we work, have a difficult time always
living the theory, or even knowing how the theory might look in
practice, is not a problem so much as an invitation. Theory, in a
sense, is similar to imagination. We have to envision the future
before we can ever hope to create it.

Point of Departure #6

Literacy always involves an intuitive leap of faith, and it is in this
leap that sign systems play a significant role.

I would like to return to the beginning. How we envision
literacy makes a difference. If we see it as meaning-making and not
meaning making plus inquiry, we see only part of what literacy can
be. I argue that literacy always involves more. We take the personal
and social meanings we have created through literacy, the familiar, to
metaphorically explain the unfamiliar.

Therefore, more is needed than just reading and discussing
the meaning of a book. The next step is to take the insights the book
holds and rethink the world. This leap is inquiry. We have a new
hypothesis, a new point of departure.

The leap from the familiar to the unfamiliar has been the
subject of many conversations in language (see Bakhtin's thinking in
Holoquist, 1990). Often, this leap is referred to as the generativeness
of language and literacy. We should perhaps think of it as why the
process of literacy is always literacy plus more. Krashen (1985) might
say, "literacy plus one." It is always possible to generate a new
perspective, to see the familiar in a new light that changes the possibilities we understand. All of a sudden we make new connections.
We see more and think differently. We have insights we lacked
before inquiring about our questions.

Sign systems, with their potential for providing multiple ways
of knowing, need to occupy the center position of curriculum. We
need sign systems to experience the full generative power of literacy,
to put an edge on everybody's learning. The authors of this book
believe the study of sign systems holds significant promise for
education. In this chapter, we have set the stage to move beyond
what has been done in the past—a trivializing of the arts. We need
not have another exercise in that. Therefore, now is the time, and

here is an invitation, to take sign systems seriously. We are fortunate in having theories that allow us to see glimmers of their potential. Take the opportunity with us, to use this theory as a lens, as we tell stories of how this theory looks in the classroom and how it allows us to better know learners challenged by our school systems.

Inquiry and Multiple Ways of Knowing in a First Grade

Beth Berghoff with Susan Hamilton

W hat have I gotten myself into now?" I wondered, as I pulled into the driveway of the dilapidated, two-story brick school. Half the windows had been replaced with now stained and dirty translucent green panels, and the parking lot, situated behind the city's juvenile detention center, was enclosed by a ten-foot high chain link fence with spirals of barbed wire on top. It seemed as if I were entering a prison, not a school. I began to wonder why I hadn't asked more questions about this place.

As I walked through the halls looking for Room 109 and Sue Hamilton, I grew a bit apprehensive. Had I made a big mistake in thinking I could come to this school and work with Sue to create a curriculum based on inquiry and multiple sign systems? I had met Sue at a summer workshop where Jerry Harste had led stimulating discussions about "multiple ways of knowing." Sue was beginning her fourth year as a first-grade teacher at this Midwestern urban elementary school. She had learned whole language theory and practice in her education courses at college, and she was doing literature study and using the authoring cycle (Harste, Short & Burke, 1988) with good success. She felt, however, that she could do more to tie her curriculum together, to make it more cohesive. She was interested in learning to plan in larger units and in doing more to make the classroom an inviting learning environment.

I was looking for a classroom where I could help the teacher design and implement a curriculum that involved inquiry and multiple sign systems. I wanted to watch the children and research their learning in such an environment. I believed I understood the theory after two years as a graduate student and had enough practical experience after seven years of elementary teaching to get such a curriculum up and running. However, I needed a partner, and while Sue seemed perfect, I wondered whether she and I had talked too much about ideas, and not enough about the school context.

"Hmmm," I mused as I stepped over missing floor tiles, "not exactly the kind of place that makes me want to sing and dance. I wonder how this rundown building impacts the kids and teachers? I guess if an inquiry and multiple ways of knowing curriculum works in this school, it will work anywhere. Room 109. I guess this is it."

Establishing a Daily Routine

When school began in the fall, I started spending three or four days a week in Sue's classroom. Before planning any units with Sue, I learned how she organized and planned for her instruction. She had established a routine that provided both structure and predictability to the day. She started the day with journal writing. The children came in, picked out their journals, and took them to their seats. They dated the page and then wrote and drew whatever they chose, knowing that after fifteen minutes or so they would join a circle on the floor and read what they had written. This morning ritual was important to the children, as evidenced by their willingness to sit quietly for all the sharing and by their enthusiasm for the writing and drawing.

Journal time was followed by a two-hour work block. The children were accustomed to using this time to read their literature, to write, and to engage in a variety of activities at centers around the room. On Monday of each week, the children chose a literature book from the selections Sue offered and, in doing so, joined a group that would work together to read and think about the book during the week. Each Friday morning, the entire work-block time was dedicated to literature projects in which the children transmediated their understandings and feelings about the books they had studied together. These transmediations took many forms—drama, costumes, murals, dioramas, puppet shows, dances, quilts, songs, story maps, and so on—and provided a rich invitation to use sign systems for expression.

Sue's morning work block was a time for small-group and individual work. The boys and girls made a lot of choices about how to proceed with their learning and were free to talk and move around as they needed. The afternoon format was a little different in that the whole class often spent time working as a group. After lunch, Sue read to them and often taught a minilesson of some sort based on the book. Next, an hour was devoted to a multiage grouping of first and second graders. Half the second graders in the adjoining class came to Sue's room, and half the first graders went next door. This provided a time when the activities could be more challenging because each first grader had a second-grade learning partner to work with. Sue used this hour for active experiences such as conducting science experiments, cooking various dishes, writing scripts, and graphing information.

Sue and I used the month of September to make plans for the Colonial America inquiry unit, which we began in early October. As a first step, we created a focused study plan for the unit (Burke, 1991). A focused study is an inquiry driven by a central question that is shared by the entire class. It is a unit of curriculum designed to involve a community of learners in the process of collaboratively constructing knowledge, as they continually seek information related to their questions from new perspectives—new sign system perspectives, new disciplinary perspectives, and new social perspectives. The in-depth nature of this kind of learning takes a significant amount of time, and the Colonial America unit was planned as a ten-week unit. We wanted the children to be able to answer the question "What was it like to live in Colonial America?"

Before starting the unit, Sue and I generated webs of concepts and connections, collected books and resources, and talked to local experts such as the art teacher and a historian. We discussed what we believed the children would connect to and the shared experiences we could have as a class. As we talked, we kept in mind the focused study framework we learned from Carolyn Burke and wrote down our ideas for learning engagements in each of the focused study categories (see Appendix A: Colonial America Focused Study).

It was interesting how the planning-to-plan process worked for us. We were not yet working together, so we found ourselves running to our notebooks and writing ideas at all times of the day. We laughed at each others' stories of sudden revelation—those moments of "Wow, we could have a portrait painter come in costume to talk to the children!" Or, "Hey, what if we cleaned out the closet and let the kids go in there to practice with the rattles and drums." These ideas seemed to hatch out of the air once we started planning, and we were glad we had agreed to have a weekly meeting to share with each other and push the process. We both found the planning more interesting and invigorating because we were working together.

As our list of possible learning engagements grew longer, we grew more deliberate in our thinking about multiple sign systems. We mentally walked through the experiences we had jotted down and asked what sign systems the children would be using. This deliberation caused us to think about how we could include more music, more art, more drama, and more movement. We also felt some pressure to be able to explain our work in terms of the essential skills established in the school curriculum, so we mapped out the proficiencies we would be teaching in each of the subject areas.

When it was time to begin teaching the unit, Sue and I switched gears a bit, and, instead of generating ideas, we began to

Figure 1.
An Example of Our
Daily Schedule

Daily Schedule

8:45   Journals
9:30   Morning Work Session
        Monday through Thursday (45 minute rotations)
        • Independent reading and writing
        • Small group discussions and instruction
        • Working at "invitations"
        Friday (no rotations—extended group work time)
        • Small groups constucting literature response projects
11:30   Whole Class Sharing or Mini-lessons
12:00   Lunch
1:00   Read Aloud
1:30   Multiage Hour
2:30   Special Classes
3:00   Learning Log Reflections
3:30   Dismissal

map out the first week's daily activities. This process forced us to discuss the daily schedule, and we decided to add two new elements: "invitations" to ensure that the children had access to many different sign systems and "learning logs" to provide daily time for reflective writing and drawing. We decided the morning work block would include three main activities and that students would rotate through these different strands in approximately forty-five- minute segments. This schedule meant that about one-third of the class would be working at "invitations"; one-third would be in a quiet part of the room reading and writing independently; and the other third would be engaged with the teacher in guided reading, literature discussion, strategy instruction, mathematics conversations, or authoring circles. Our daily schedule is shown in Figure 1.

The three-strand structure of invitations, teacher-directed small-group work, and independent reading and writing time worked so well that we continued it throughout the entire school year. We also maintained the practice of taking time at the end of the day to stop and have the children write and draw in a learning log. This activity afforded them the chance to record what they learned on any one day and to begin to see connections across the unit of study. As an assessment tool, the learning logs provided us with a good measure of the students' progress. We gained important insight into what the children found significant and how they fit new information into their existing schema. We also learned that the children

Figure 2.
Molly's Conceptualization
of the Learning Process

worked at conceptualizing their own learning. Entries such as
Molly's (Figure 2) showed us that our students were not only constructing understandings of Colonial American life and times but
they were also learning about learning.

We loved Molly's entry because it showed us how she managed parallel intellectual processes—the internal construction going
on in her head and the external recording going on as she drew a
representation of what she was thinking. Molly, a first grader, taught
us that drawing is equally as powerful as language. She understood
learning in ways she could never articulate in words, yet her drawing gave us access to her thinking and offered us new ways to
imagine her as a learner.

Building Multiple Ways of Knowing into Invitation Time

Adding invitation time to the daily schedule also turned out to be an amazing experience. We used the term "invitations" to refer to open-ended learning activities designed for small groups or individuals to work on independent of the teacher. Each invitation consisted of a variety of materials such as art supplies, mathematics manipulatives, or dress-up clothes; resources such as books, art prints, videotapes, or audiotapes; and simple, brief, start-up directions or questions to consider. We learned from Carolyn Burke to give each invitation a jazzy, yet conceptual, title that could become a shorthand way of talking about the learning experiences as a class. We wrote the titles on signs or folders to mark the location of each invitation in the classroom. Our classroom was large enough that we could locate several invitations around the perimeter of the room, and we positioned them so that each invitation included a specific work area. Once an invitation had been introduced, it remained available until the children lost interest in it. Some invitations remained popular for weeks; others lasted only a few days.

As we introduced new invitations, we made a conscious effort to demonstrate some of the ways the media and tools belonging to different sign systems might be used. For example, Sue introduced "The Quilt Invitation" by laying out several patterns with blocks and talking about the patterns. Next, she laid out a pattern with blocks and replicated the pattern with fabric squares. Finally, she had the children look for the patterns in handmade quilts and pictures of quilts. The invitation to the students required they either use fabric, scissors, and glue to create patterns that matched patterns they found in other quilts or make up their own patterns that might produce interesting quilts. We provided a set of picture books about quilts, along with a couple of small doll quilts and boxes of material scraps and pattern blocks.

As we observed the children during the quilt invitation, we learned a great deal about them. None of the children copied the patterns they saw in other quilts. Some laid out simple patterns of their own; others pasted material scraps together without patterns. In some cases, their coordination lagged behind their patterning ability. They could not cut fabric to the exact size and shape they wanted, so they focused on the patterns of color and design in the fabric rather than on patterns of shape. One child started taping her pattern of fabric pieces to the wall beside the invitation and asking her peers to describe the pattern they saw. Other students added to this initial pattern, and eventually there was a quilt of many different patterns on the wall. This quilt inspired some wonderful mathematics conversations. Still other students, Monica, for example, focused on the patterns in the fabrics and used the patterns they observed to invent their own.

Figure 3.
Monica's Quilt from
Her Own Patterns

Initial experiences such as this patterning practice prompted the children to think differently—broader, more encompassing—about new elements introduced at the invitation. After a time, we introduced *The Quilt* (Jonas, 1984), a picture book the children could read to each other about a girl who enters the world of the quilt on her bed when she dreams at night. The children had to closely observe the quilt in the illustrations to discover the source of the dream images. We knew they understood the story because we offered tempera paints and a firm fabric to paint on, and this time the children made representational quilt squares—sailboats, suns, rainbows, flowers, and so on. This new media changed what they could do, and the book changed what they were thinking about in relationship to quilts. Throughout the unit, we continued to introduce new picture books and media to The Quilt Center. When we finally discussed women quilting in Colonial American times, we encouraged the children to connect to the experiences and concepts they had developed through The Quilt Center.

In our planning, we viewed the invitations as part of the "wandering and wondering" (Burke & Short, 1995) our learners needed to do to understand the territory of our shared inquiry question and to arrive at their own personal inquiry questions. We also thought of the invitations as social learning opportunities. By offering invitation time to only a third of the class at a time, we could afford to encourage the children to work in pairs or small groups and to talk, act, play music, or construct items quietly at the invitations. With only six to nine children moving around at a time, the room remained quiet and calm enough for the rest of the learners to work in more structured ways. The learners could make choices because there were always other open invitations, and we put them in charge of deciding when they were productively engaged and when they were finished.

Learning about Learners through Invitations

The children engaged in conversations as they worked at invitations, and these conversations comprised an important part of their learning. Videotaping the students allowed me to listen in on some of these conversations more carefully—thus enabling me to appreciate the way the children made connections and constructed meaning by zigzagging between their use of the media and materials, other parts of their lives, and the sensory aspects of their experiences. This exchange between Charles and Juanita illustrates the kind of connective chatter we often saw.

Our shared reading about Native Americans had mentioned that they appreciated the beauty of their natural world and created art by using dyes extracted from plants. This led to our experimenting with boiling items the children predicted would create color— yellow squash peelings, blueberries, spinach, and so forth. "The Natural Dyes" invitation consisted of a table covered in newspaper, large manilla paper, small containers of watery "dye," and paint brushes.

The video segment began with Charles and Juanita standing side by side and just starting to paint. Two other students, Chris and Romien, were watching the painters, somewhat reluctant to move on to their own activities.

Chris:	(*Looking at the curve of Charles's first paint strokes.*) What's that?
Romien:	It's a wigwam, ain't it Charles?
Charles:	No.
Chris:	What is it?
Charles:	Rainboooooooow.
Sue:	(*She has noticed the extra people at the invitation and asks:*) How many people belong at that center?
Chris and Romien:	Two. (*The boys recognize Sue's question as a signal to move to a different invitation. They move elsewhere, leaving Charles and Juanita alone at the table.*)

Charles: (*To himself.*) It ain't no wigwam. It's a rainbow. (*Enjoying the sound of the words as he makes concentric half circles with his brush on the paper.*)

Charles: (*As he dips into the bowl of yellowish water left from boiling crookneck squash, says to Juanita:*) This is made out of water. Is this water?

Juanita: No.

Charles: What is it?

Juanita: It's squash.

Charles: Well, I'm going to eat it.

Juanita: It's squash and juice.

Charles: And can we eat it?

Juanita: Ugh . . . then we'd be eating off a paint brush.

Charles: (*Leans his head down to the bowl and acts as if he has slurped juice from his brush.*) Ugh . . . that's nasty.

Both children focus again on their painting. Juanita is concentrating on details and painting in small strokes. Charles watches her for a second.

Charles: That ain't how you paint.

Juanita: So.

Charles: You don't know how to paint. This is how you paint. (*He demonstrates by filling his brush full of the dye and sweeping it from one edge of the paper to the other, imitating a housepainter. He becomes absorbed in the motion and says, more to himself than to Juanita:*) This is how my Daddy paints. Except he paints way more faster.

Juanita: (*Leaning over Charles's paper to see how his technique is working.*) You got a lot of paint. There's a lot of paint on here.

Charles: (*Looking, in turn, at Juanita's painting.*) Yours is dryin'. (*He touches the manila paper, which has absorbed most of the watery color.*) It is dry.

Both children concentrate on painting again for awhile, and then Charles picks up one of the bowls of dye and pretends to drink from it.

Juanita: Hey that's squash. (*She takes the bowl from his hands and puts it back in place on the table.*)

Charles: I'm gonna drink some. Give me that. (*He reaches for the bowl and notices that Annie is watching him from the next table. He says to her:*) I drank some of the water, some of that.

Annie: *I thought one person can only be there.*

Charles: You can be at this center because, look, it's almost dry. . . . (*He has his finger on Juanita's paper, but it is not as dry as he expected.*) . . . never mind.

Juanita: (*Getting a little impatient with Charles's intrusion.*) So it don't mean nothing. When I get done at the center, Annie, you can come work here.

Annie: I don't want to.

Juanita: Oh.

They concentrate again on painting. One of the paint bowls is a glass custard dish. Each time Charles dips into the paint, he flips the metal tip of his brush from side to side and produces a series of clear, high-pitched clinks. He gets very involved in the sound and the movement and continues making the sound for several seconds.

Juanita: Now I'm all out. (*Juanita has used most of the blueberry dye.*)

Charles: (*Picks up the bottle with the squash dye he is using.*) Let me pour this in.

Juanita: That's the same as this.

Charles: I know. I gotta pour a little. Don't I? Could I?

Juanita: (*Shakes her head no.*)

Charles puts the jar of extra squash dye down and uses his brush to soak up the last of the blueberry dye while Juanita is using the squash dye.

Juanita: Now my last . . . Oh boy, you took all of it.

Charles: (*Reaching past Juanita to use the spinach dye.*) I'm almost finished with this.

Juanita: (*Attempting to lift the spinach dye and move it toward Charles.*) Here.

Charles: (*Dripping dye on Juanita's hand.*) Better move.

Juanita: Oh boy. . . . (*She steps back to dry her hand.*)

Charles: (*Still painting, breaks into a rap.*)
Oh boy, I'm talking to M.C. Hammer.
Yeah sure. Come on,
Come on and talk to him.
M.C. Ham-, M.C. Ham-

(*Assuming a different voice and stance.*) Oh, paa-leeeease!

As Charles dips again into the dye, he stirs it vigorously for several seconds, obviously enjoying the rhythm of the clinking metal on glass.

Juanita: Don't do that Charles.

Charles: Why? (*He stops and considers again the possibility of opening the jar of extra dye.*) We need some more, don't we? In this one?

Juanita: (*Trying to reach over Charles to get to the dye.*) Can you excuse me?

Charles: Nope.

Juanita: Can you move that over there?

Juanita finishes and puts her name on her painting, then carries it off to lay it on the windowsill where it will dry. Charles lifts his painting carefully. The water-soaked manila paper is extra flexible. He places it wet-side down on the table so he can paint his name on the back.

Charles: Mine's dry. (*He lays the paper on the windowsill.*)

Invitations, unlike worksheets or seatwork, encouraged the kind of running dialogue that Charles and Juanita engaged in at the Natural Dyes invitation. The conversations that took place at the invitations helped us to understand that learning was much more about connecting to things that were in the children's experience and negotiating social positions than we were thinking it was. In this instance, Juanita felt very responsible for doing things the right way. She tolerated Charles and communicated a seriousness about the work that helped to keep him on track. She was fairly oblivious to his critical comments and did not respond to his antagonistic moves. She made her social connections with Annie by extending an offer to give Annie her spot at the invitation when she was finished.

Charles, on the other hand, was more of a free spirit. His talk linked the world of school to the world outside school. He reflected on how his father painted and relived a little drama connected to a rap song he had heard. Charles was very tactile, touching the wet papers repeatedly to check his perception of wetness and clinking the paintbrush against the glass. He considered tasting the paints and even acted as if he had tasted some to see what kind of response he elicited. Lucky for us, Juanita was there to gently instill a sense of limits and acceptable behavior.

Over the course of the year, Sue and I developed a deep appreciation for invitations because we learned such very important things about our learners by watching them at work with media other than academic language. For example, we learned that all of our learners demonstrated persistence and concentration when they found an activity that met their interest and developmental needs. We had several children who struggled some with reading and writing. They often lost interest in print-focused work quickly, but they would stay at "The Reflection Center," where they could construct props for their dramas, hard at work for a full forty-five-minute invitation rotation. Or, they would spend their entire invitation time drawing a self-portrait, creating a Venn diagram, or acting out a part. As a result of these choices, the slower learners never suffered the same social stigma many children do when they lag behind the others in their development of reading and writing. They produced projects that were worthy of admiration, just in a media other than print. The class did not assign social standing on the basis of literacy.

Even though the invitations were only available to the children for a small part of the day, the opportunity to shift and think in a variety of sign systems seemed to change the dynamics of the entire day. Children would plan ahead, "You guys, we can act out this story tomorrow." Or, "I want to work with you tomorrow at the Museum." Some children returned to the same invitation every day for weeks. Others never did the same thing two days in a row. Children such as Monica used invitation time for personal explorations. Monica created her own notation for writing the song she composed at the keyboard. Other children made their choices about what to do based more on those with whom they would be working rather than on the engagement itself.

The best invitations took on a life of their own. While the children usually began their work at invitations according to Sue's demonstrations and suggestions, their deeper involvement with the media often opened up new possibilities to them. They would find new purposes for using the invitations and invent new ways to use the media and tools. As we watched, we could support these shifts and add new tools or demonstrations to make the invitations responsive to the students' interests and learning. For example, the Colonial America unit featured a museum invitation. This invitation consisted of a stand-up Peg-Board hung with artifacts that resembled those used in the era when our country was new—pieces of rabbit pelt, wooden spoons, shells, dried corn, and so on. Initially, we invited the children to act only as museum curators and to write labels and descriptive accounts of how the artifacts might have been used. Later, as they became interested in sorting the items, we added two huge yarn circles they could lay out on the floor to make a Venn diagram, and they sorted items into categories such as Pilgrim and Native American artifacts. They also began to use the artifacts to act out the stories we were reading to the class, so we added a costumes invitation that encouraged more of this kind of drama.

In November, when I recorded in my field notes what was going on in the room, the invitations consisted of a museum with real artifacts to sort and label (encouraging dramatic play, language, and drawing); a wigwam with dress-up clothes (drama); an invitation to paint with natural dyes made from boiled spinach, squash, and onions (visual art); a portrait center with a display of period art and an easel for drawing (visual art); a flannel board with Pilgrim and number cutouts (mathematics); and a closet with drums, rattles, and poetry (music). There was also a listening center with tapes and recorders, a library corner, a computer, a musical keyboard, a writing center, and a reflection/art center. These centers were always available as well. It looked as follows:

> There is a pegboard at one end of the room hung with articles such as Indian corn, fur, deer antlers, wooden utensils, a bellows, and quilts. A felt sign with block letters says MUSEUM, and two girls are moving the hooks and rearranging the collection of items. One child explains to the other that shells were all the Indians had for silverware and demonstrates how she would scoop up food with a big clam shell. Together they read through a pile of hand-lettered labels written by their classmates and find the one with "shel." It gets taped up beside the shells.
>
> Nearby stands a large dome structure made of tent poles and partially covered with orange and brown mats of woven paper. Many have mistakenly called this a tepee, only to be corrected by the children who know about different kinds of Indian homes. It is a wigwam and the children inside have on long skirts and buckskin. They are pretending to be Squanto and the Pilgrims. Karen, one of the Pilgrim women, offers Squanto a quilt in hopes that he will trade the rabbit fur and corn he has brought into the wigwam in a basket. He picks kernels off the corncob as he considers the offer, and then nods. Almost repeating the exact words he has heard from the story of Squanto read to the class, he says, "Tomorrow I will show you how to plant corn with fish."
>
> "Yeah," says Karen. "That's what you do. So then we won't be so hungry."
>
> Molly groans, "I'm hungry, Mom." And the drama goes on.
>
> Sue is on the floor with the small group of children who have chosen to read The Oxcart Man, and a few children are at their desks, reading to themselves or writing. No one is painting with natural dyes at a table by the windows, drawing a personal portrait, or creating story problems using flannel cutouts of the Mayflower and Pilgrims, but Leonard is in the closet reading poetry and patting out rhythms on a small drum.
>
> In a few minutes, Sue calls for a switch. The children who have been reading and talking with her go to work at their seats while members of the group who were up bring their books and come to the circle on the floor. Those who were at their desks begin negotiating with each other about what areas to work in. During the course of the morning, they will move three times—to reading and writing at their seats, literature circle with Sue, and invitations.

Invitations solved one of our challenges in creating multiple ways of knowing curriculum, because they enabled us to set up an environment that made multiple sign systems available to the children. They also allowed us to begin with what we knew about art, music, drama, and movement and then learn from watching the children. Drama was one of these fertile learning strands. When we began, we had no idea how much the children would use drama to push their understandings. Over the course of the year, the children's use of drama changed drastically. Initially, they were not very deliberate about drama. It happened spontaneously when they put on costumes or imagined a story together. As they experienced this spontaneous drama, however, they began to be more purposeful in making drama represent a particular story. Parts were assigned, someone narrated the story line, and props were used to set the scene. This led into improvisational drama where the actors started in one story, but negotiated along the way to add new dimensions and invent a new story. All of this was coupled with changes in their ability to convey messages. They learned about staging and involving the audience, about movement and qualities of voice. Some of them became quite respected as dramatic actors or actresses, while others perfected their comedic talents. All of this was possible because of potentials inherent in the learning environment. Sue and I did not know enough about drama to set out purposefully on this journey, but we could respond to what we saw happening and continue to support the children's use of drama to think about what they were learning.

Music provided another rich learning strand for us. We set up very basic music invitations. In one corner of the room, the children could compose on an electric keyboard. Headphones made the music audible to only the child who was playing. In another corner, we had a table full of materials for making shakers and rattles. We also cleaned out a closet and let the children sit inside it to practice ostinatos (rhythm patterns) and play along with the beat in poems and recorded music. We were able to observe children composing music and creating their own notation systems. We also had children borrowing music and inserting it into their dramas and presentations. The diversity of music we provided acted as a bridge to the children's home cultures. Louise and Molly felt comfortable bringing their violins to school; Leonard and Charles felt comfortable breakdancing to a rap version of the song "Who's Afraid of the Big Bad Wolf"; and Monica was willing to perform a song from "Annie" after attending the show.

Incorporating a Cycle of Personal Inquiry

Our focused study plan was our plan for creating a shared inquiry unit. By consciously supporting the process of "wandering and wondering" through literature choices, read alouds, writing projects, invitations, and demonstrations, we introduced rich new information and provided many means for processing that information so that the children were making connections and doing conceptual-level thinking. By the time we reached the sixth week of the Colonial America focused study, the children were explaining the time period with stories about specific people such as Squanto, a Native American, and Sarah Morton, a fictional Pilgrim child. They were aware of the kinds of things people had to do in their daily lives to survive and knew information about the homes and lifestyles of the Native Americans and the Pilgrims. Had our unit ended at this point in time, it would have been successful in its own right; however, we wanted to go a step further and expose the children to inquiry as a personal learning process. The six weeks of inquiry as an entire class set the stage for meaningful individual questions related to the focused study.

Since Colonial America was our first collaborative inquiry unit, we gave much thought to explaining the process and providing support for the learners. We decided that each of our students would pursue a personal question, and afterward we would group them together to plan their final presentations. We wanted to avoid over-whelming them in this introduction to inquiry, plus we knew the groups would provide social learning support.

We moved slowly through the question-generating step, asking the students one day just to share the questions on their minds about Colonial America. We filled a chart paper with questions. With these questions in mind, Sue and I pulled together as many books and magazines and other resources as we could that seemed to address the questions generated by the children. We encouraged the children to browse through the resources and to think about a question they would like to pursue for themselves. Again we wrote these on chart paper, only this time, there was one question for each child.

As the class studied the list of specific questions, Sue helped them look for connections among the questions so that the students could work in small groups. The children saw connections and helped with identifying groups. They also pointed out specific resources that would help individuals with their questions.

At this point, we had to look beyond our class for help because most of these first graders were not yet able to read many of the texts that we had collected. Therefore, we decided to make an inquiry journal for each student by stapling blank pieces of paper together and having the students print their inquiry questions on the front. Next, we sent each child home with a bag that contained the inquiry journal and a resource book or two that was likely to help with his or her question. We sent a note in the bag asking the parents or some older person to 1) talk with the child about his or her question and write notes in the inquiry journal about what the student already knew about the question; and 2) read the books in the bag to the student and together record the pertinent new information by writing or drawing (either parent or child) in the inquiry journal. In the best cases, the children returned in a few days with inquiry journals like Christopher's, as shown in Figure 4.

Figure 4.
Christopher's
Inquiry Journal

Figure 4. Christopher's Inquiry Journal

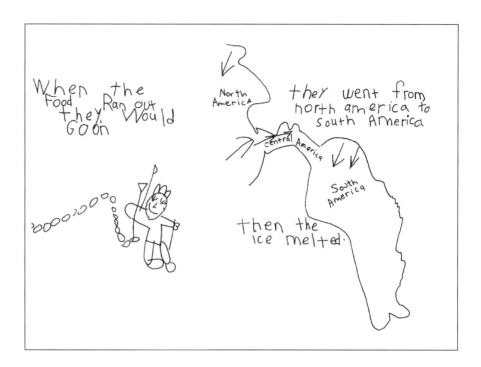

When the
Food they Ran out Would
Go on

North
America

they went from
north america to
south America

Central America

South
America

then the
ice melted.

the sea came up higher
and covered the land
bridge

No one else could come
to the America's like the
Indians

ASIA

When Sue and I studied the inquiry journals, we noticed that most of the students knew a lot about their questions. In fact, most knew so much that they could already answer their questions at some level before they started their inquiry. At first, we believed we had moved too quickly to formulating questions. In hindsight, however, we reflected that we personally operated in the same way as our students. After we thought about our own inquiry experiences, we realized that we too asked questions that we knew something about. Just as the first graders, we too chose to focus our energy on what we thought we could verify or understand at a deeper level. We realized that good inquiry must begin with abundant prior knowledge. Starting from a well-developed conceptual framework made it easier to recognize when new information was not fitting the schema or adding to what was already known and understood.

Once all the inquiry journals were back at school, Sue turned literature-circle time into inquiry-group time and had the students bring their journals and books to the teacher-directed sessions during the morning work block. The children shared what they had learned and transferred the information to chart paper, graffiti style, so they could get a larger view of what they shared. They discussed their questions, their knowledge, and the connections. Next, Sue worked with them to decide what new information needed to be shared with the entire class and how they could do that sharing. With her help, each small group planned a presentation for the class and for about three days, the whole class prepared for presentations, creating scripts, dioramas, charts, plays, play dough representations, quilts, and murals.

At last, presentation day arrived and each group took its turn in front while the other students sat on the floor. Sue established the pattern for sharing. First, the group members gave their presentation and exhibited their artifacts without interruption. Next, the group members could call on two or three members of the audience to talk about something they liked about the presentation. Finally, the group could call on students who raised their hands to ask questions about the information presented. Each group stayed up front until the conversation between the audience and group members ended.

This first round of sharing was nervous and tentative, but as the year progressed, the presentations became much more elaborate and interactive and students in the audience began to ask better and better questions of their classmates.

As a culmination to the Colonial America unit, the children charted their group answer to the question "What was life like in Colonial America?" They put together personal portfolios and invited their families to pitch in an authentic Thanksgiving dinner. It was a grand celebration. The parents were led around to all the inquiry exhibits, and the presentations were repeated over and over.

Literacy from the Perspective of Multiple Ways of Knowing

In creating a curriculum based on multiple ways of knowing, we aimed to support learners in developing wide-ranging sensibilities and in communicating in complex ways. While we did not know at the outset exactly what that might look like, we began to recognize it as we watched the children toward the end of the school year. Remarkably, they had developed a willingness to prolong literacy engagements and to create deeper, more complex meanings using multiple sign systems. Take, for example, Gina's reading of *Snail's Spell* (Ryder, 1982). On the morning after she had read the book, Gina could hardly wait to get into the classroom—arriving several minutes before any of the other children. She made a fairly dramatic entry, and she struggled to get her backpack unzipped, to hang it on the closet hook, and to pull her book out—all at the same time. Sue watched with amusement and asked, "Gina, how did you get in here so quickly?"

"I made my legs walk their fastest walk," Gina responded and headed for Sue's desk with her book in hand. "I want to read this book to the class!" she exhaled in spurts, holding the book for Sue to see. "And I know just what activity to do with it."

Gina explained to Sue that the children would be invited to act like the snail in the book as she read it to them. Sue agreed that Gina should read the book and carry out her plan for the class during the sharing time after lunch.

During her morning reading and writing time, Gina read the book to herself. When she came to literature study group later in the morning, she brought *Snail's Spell* along with the book her group was reading. She told Sue, "I just can't think about any other book but this one."

When sharing time finally came, Gina situated herself on a chair and had the children sit on the floor in front of her. She paired them off and explained that one member of each pair would be the lettuce leaf at the end of the story. She then instructed them to "think and act like a snail." As she read the book, she had the children shrinking, squirming prone on the floor, putting out their antennae, and wrapping their bodies around the lettuce leaf. The writhing bodies of her classmates were totally absorbed in being snails and the end of the book came too soon. They talked Gina into reading it again, this time so they could see the pictures as she read.

After the sharing time, Gina told me that the reading didn't go exactly as she had imagined it, but that was fine with her. "Everyone does things a little differently," she said. She seemed satisfied, and she was planning to take the book home to do the "activity" with her brother.

We interpreted Gina's reading as multiple ways of knowing because of the many sign systems and layers of meaning she was able to bring into connection with the book. Her reading involved more than making meaning from the language and pictures of the book. She also imagined a drama rich in sensory experience and imagined her classmates performing the drama. This extended the time she spent with the book and the attention she gave to the pictures and words. She reflected about how her classmates' performance compared to her envisionment of the "activity," and decided that she would readily try it all again in another context.

Changes in the Classroom

Sue, the first graders, and I finished the school year with a study that focused on "What's real? What's make-believe?" We worked until the last possible minute of school, making a video tape of the children's final inquiry presentations. The obvious excitement and intellectual engagement in our classroom stood in stark contrast to the classrooms around us where the books were being put away, and the children were playing games and cleaning desks—both teachers and students waiting to be set free. As we stripped the walls, the students reclaimed their artwork, graphs, and writing and created an illustrated time-line of our journey across the year. They packed more into their portfolios and asked if the "Big Bang" inquiry group could present their demonstration again after lunch. For these students, there was no sense of drudgery or longing for release. School had meaning, and it was meaning they personally helped to construct.

Sue and I knew that we had children among the group of eighteen students who would have looked very different in a different classroom context. The kindergarten teacher often asked us about three boys in particular, children she had labeled "the three Musketeers" when she had them in class. We suspect she did not believe us when we continued to tell her that they were doing fine, because she finally came to visit our classroom for an hour during the last week of school. She could scarcely believe that the independent, self-directed learners she observed in our classroom were the same children. She later told us that she felt as if she had walked into another world.

In some ways, Sue and I also felt as if we had entered a new world. The students who arrived at Room 109 each day were a diverse and challenging group. However, the learning community that developed over the year provided them with a sense of security as well as agency for their own learning. Each child was respected for his or her strengths, but also expected to do his or her part on behalf of the learning community.

The simple changes we had made—planning collaborative inquiry units, using invitations to incorporate multiple sign systems, and devoting daily time to reflective thinking—made a tremendous difference in the ways we knew our learners. We understood their learning patterns and beliefs in detail because we saw them using such a variety of sign systems to think and learn. We could see how each child's personal theory of learning impacted every experience. And we were beginning to see how experience with one way of knowing paved the way for breakthroughs in another. This understanding made it much easier for us to support the development of all the children. We had only one boy who was still struggling with print literacy at the end of the year, but this child, who said in October that he did not like coming to school because he could not read, left us believing he was a reader and writer. At a center where he was invited to choose a photograph and to write about it, he chose a picture of himself writing and wrote: "I am riten [sic] because I am learning." He chose another picture of himself reading and commented, "I am reading because I can learn to read."

As teachers, we grew to trust the children's choices in new ways. We delighted in their generative ideas for new projects, for example, a picture-book story of the modern Cinderella who went to the ball at the White House and the drama that incorporated several fairy tales as well as real life experiences. We knew from the children's written reflections that they had reasons for their choices and often recognized what would be most beneficial to them personally.

After the children had gone for the summer, I was sorting through photocopies I had made of their final projects and found Brittney's poetry book. In her note about the author on the back of the book, I felt that she had summed up the ethos of the class (Figure 5). The children knew they were learners, and they knew they learned by "doing" and "seeing" and sharing—a first-grade description of the inquiry process. They were aware of changes in themselves and extended invitations to each other to learn together. Brittney's language for expressing all this may have been less than perfect, but her message was clear.

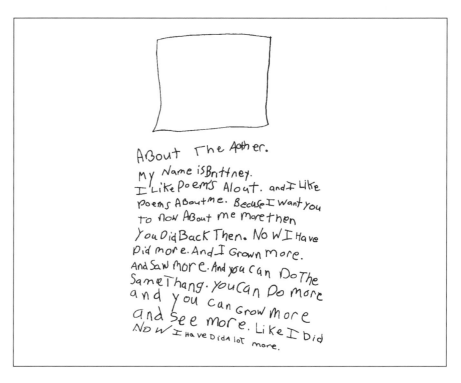

About the Author
My name is Brittney.
I like poems a lot.
And I like poems about me,
because I want you to know more about me then you did back then.
Now I have did more and I have grown more and saw more.
And you can do the same thing.
You can do more and you can grow more and see more like I did.
Now I have did a lot more.

Scott

Kathryn A. Egawa

Arts in the Classroom— Where I Began

I first began my journey into inquiry and multiple ways of knowing when I consciously realized that I treated "the arts" superficially. Across the years, as a first-grade teacher, I valued that my students' art work differed from one another's, that it did not look alike—and I was appalled when one of my fellow teachers held up a student's piece of art to demonstrate a "bad" example. I was confident that I would never do that. But, certainly, I didn't do much in the name of art that now seems significant. Like many teachers, the classroom time I allotted to art was usually reserved for Friday afternoons—a series of one-hour "projects" that I initiated or a "free choice" art time. The songs we sang were the ones I'd chosen. The dances were choreographed by others. The daily art accompanied writing assignments, and I boldly requested *no* background around the large, painted pumpkins and large, fuschia-colored hearts that I intended to cut out and use to decorate the room.

Nonetheless, the kids worked around my taken-for-granted views. Here and there, I found scraps of paper on the floor, notes and pictures for friends, or favorite picture books tucked in desks. Discovery of this classroom subculture, whose membership excluded me, prompted me to begin asking kids about their own ideas. This new stance positioned me to truly begin learning from the young members of our classroom community. What I had previously been doing had little to do with what I now understand about sign systems. Nonetheless, I could say that these experiences presented me with the opportunity to learn more. The kids had a lot to teach me!

Taking a New Look

My "learning more" escalated during a year-long collaboration with a university colleague, Ray Roussin. Ray kept free one morning a week to work in my classroom, and we focused our energy on literature study. We shifted our curricular emphasis from a traditional reading program to, what was then new, literature discussion groups. Shifting this focus—from an established reading curriculum to one building on kids' own ideas—set me up to learn in new and exciting ways.

We invited the kids to express their ideas and to spend their time in a variety of ways. As a result, they created art using methods I hadn't before emphasized: they improvised costumes, created murals, and painted what a story meant to them. As they worked, they talked animatedly about the story lines of their books. Did the hen ever know the fox was following behind her (*Rosie's Walk*)? Should She-Who-Was-Alone have thrown her doll in the fire to acknowledge it as her most precious belonging (*The Legend of Bluebonnet*)? Is the child who goes owling with dad a girl or a boy (*Owl Moon*)?

One particular moment stands out for me. Before his group's presentation of *Chicken Soup with Rice,* Eric quietly tiptoed over to me and asked, "Is it okay if I dance my presentation?" Initially I congratulated myself, thinking, "Wow, isn't that a great question! Isn't this a great class!" but then I later thought, "Isn't it odd that he felt he had to *ask* me if he could dance?" Despite all the good things that were going on, my perspective on the role of "the arts" had changed very little. I was learning, though, to listen to the ideas of my students in ways that, admittedly, I never had before. Making significant changes in the curriculum had opened up new possibilities for their responses.

Later that year, I attended a regional NCTE conference and heard Jerry Harste speak. Not only was he the most outrageous speaker I'd ever heard but he was also a creative, innovative, and inspiring teacher who took a theoretical perspective. For the first time in my career I was listening to someone talk about curriculum in ways that resonated with my experience. Eager to be part of such thinking, I was soon on my way to Indiana University to study with him and Carolyn Burke.

Putting New Theoretical Knowledge into Practice

When I left for graduate school, after eighteen years of teaching, I was only beginning to understand how much my students could facilitate their own learning; I needed to get further out of their way, especially during their work times. There was more, however, to understanding the importance of music, drama, and art than just moving out of their way. I had to create not only a context in which they could explore their own ideas as readers and writers but also an atmosphere where their ideas mattered, where they could ask, "But why can't we do it this way?" My work with Ray had helped me put away many of my taken-for-granted notions of schooling and embrace a more-encompassing definition of learning.

In 1993, after four years of graduate school, I pushed myself to coalesce these many experiences and to much more consciously impact curriculum. My understanding of "the arts" had shifted to a theoretical understanding of sign systems, and I asked myself what this new knowledge could do for me as a teacher. What did I now have the potential to see that I couldn't have seen before?

To answer these questions, I first had to consider where, and with whom, I worked. I interviewed at a school known for its focus on language arts and the arts, led by a principal who valued and recruited teacher-leaders. The music teacher was a performing musician; one of the fourth-grade teachers directed children's theater; and Barry Hoonan had come to the same school several years before with a rich background in children's poetry and literature. He had initiated weekly student-led assemblies—and in the span of a couple years, these became productions that one would expect to see once a year in an elementary school. This school community valued new thinking and challenges; I was excited to once again be working with young students and with an engaged group of educators.

The Challenge Takes a Personal Face

Two weeks into the school year, Scott entered my classroom—and in him I found the challenge that pushed me to really think about what I'd learned. Scott's second-grade teacher knew of my background in literacy, recognized Scott's struggles, and transferred him into my classroom at a time when large class sizes necessitated creating a multiage classroom.

I received one of my first impressions of Scott through his writing. Figure 1, a sample from the dialogue journal I kept with each student, shows his limited experience as a writer. One might expect this level of understanding and control of written language in the fall or winter of the first grade—at the latest—but not in the second grade.

Figure 1.
Sample from Scott's
Dialogue Journal

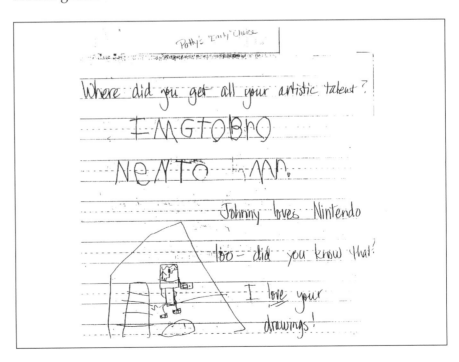

Based on his journal, I recognized Scott as a "beginning writer" (Campbell Hill & Ruptic/4, 1997), but that impression of him broadened as I noticed his talents in other areas of the curriculum. While browsing through the students' work after school, I ran across this drawing in his sketch pad. As one of many possibilities for the students' sketching, I had suggested they sketch any of the songs we sang; Scott had illustrated the entire landscape of *The Fox*, as shown in Figure 2. I could make out the farm, the chicken pen, the hill where John trumpeted his warning, and the foxes' den. Never before had I seen a primary-aged student take such a landscape perspective in a drawing. Scott caught my attention, and I began to look more closely at his work.

Figure 2.
Scott's Illustration of *The Fox*

Soon after noting his sketch, I began a second round of "getting-to-know-you" activities (Harste, Short & Burke, 1988); Scott was one of twelve students who entered our class two weeks into the school year; consequently, we needed a chance to reestablish our classroom community. As Scott introduced us to favorite items in his "cool-stuff box," I learned that his most intense personal interest was jets. Again, he had caught my attention, and predictably, when I walked over to him at work, or took a moment to look through his sketch pad, images of jets showed up (Figure 3). I assembled these examples from different pages over several months. The sophistication of ideas and discipline, not yet evident in his writing, could be found in his sketches.

Figure 3.
Scott's Drawings of Jets

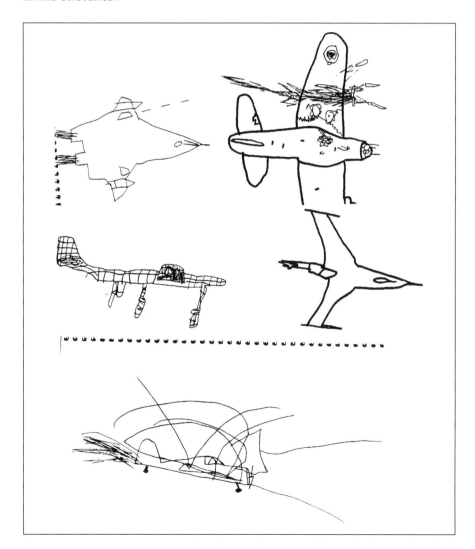

Unlike many less-capable students, Scott was engaged and collaborative in the classroom. He often chose to write with a friend, and he selected friends who would take the lead in getting their ideas down on paper. His buddy reading time was spent with books, and he often read the pictures while his buddy read the text. He seldom spent time with simple texts, as one might expect from a beginning reader; he gravitated instead to the technical, sophisticated texts in our class library. More often than not, the books focused on jets.

When Scott's buddy reading group cycled to the "meet-with-the-teacher" table, I better understood his picture browsing. Scott had apparently learned that reading was a laborious process of sounding out words. In my many years of teaching, I had never heard a reader like him. He dissected the words stiffly, slowly, and in a very exaggerated manner. My student teacher even called me aside and whispered, "*What* is he doing?" I didn't know where he had learned this behavior. I guessed, though, that someone at home might have been encouraging him to "sound out" words. Scott's mother came in to meet me, and she assured me that Scott hadn't learned such behavior at home. I realized the assumption I'd made; nevertheless, I was pleased for the chance to meet her and to share some strategies to support him.

Scott's reading did improve as I introduced him to books with predictable patterns. When he read with me, I focused on reading smoothly along with him; consequently, most of the jerkiness fell away. His repertoire of favorite books grew larger, yet his first choice remained nonfiction that challenged his reading ability.

From the Invitation Corner

Over time, Scott came to my attention in other ways as well. In October, I noticed repeated strands of "Wild Thing" coming from the invitation corner of the classroom. The students went there for self-directed learning experiences, often related to class inquiries. Musical instruments filled the shelves alongside art materials, tools, sewing supplies, and costumes. Scott was a beginning piano player, and "Wild Thing" had been a favorite in his lessons. With the opportunity to direct his own choices, he often played the song on an Orff xylophone and had then taught it to a number of his classmates. Someone had even attached a scrap of paper with some notes to a nearby poster. I brought in some music paper for Scott and suggested he write out how to play it—an idea inspired by the work of colleagues (Harste, Woodward & Burke, 1984; Levi, 1993). Figure 4 shows Scott's invented notation.

Of all the activity centers, it was the invitation area that most engaged the students' interests. Nicole enjoyed dance, music, and art. She worked for months to capture movement in her sketches and

Figure 4.
Scott's Invented Notation
of "Wild Thing"

then reworked the best of them in watercolor. Johnny and Christy also liked drawing and often combined this interest with their interest in animals. Sets of hard rubber animals (whales, turtles, snakes, wolves) and picture books were paired with directions to create realistic habitats. The two of them worked on several turtle habitats for days. Dane liked drama and often gathered his friends to make up stories and props. Hannah, Mitchell, and Maxwell could always be found with the tools and broken small appliances. The shift to a curriculum centered around inquiry helped me know kids' interests in ways I never had before. Their interests mattered both inside and outside the classroom.

A special component of the curriculum that year, facilitated by my student teacher's requisite month of teaching, was a series of four field trips. I arranged trips I knew would capture their interests and invited the kids to sign up—six kids, me, and a parent for each trip. Scott was absent on the day we signed up, so his classmates selected him for the visit to the Potlatch exhibit at the Seattle Art Museum, arguing that he'd been to the Flight Museum many times already. They knew that his specific interest, which came out in our second round of inquiry projects, included bows and arrows and the speed at which arrows travel.

On the day of our visit, Scott walked quickly into the exhibit area, opened up his sketch pad, and started sketching. For an hour he walked from display to display, not talking with anyone, drawing the items that captured his attention. Figure 5 shows some of his work from that day.

As I watched Scott hard at work that day, I remember thinking that none of us—educators or parents—could afford to view a student such as Scott as unsuccessful. He knew so much and was so engaged as a learner; yet at the time, he was also a second grader who was a much less-capable reader and writer than most of his peers. His focused drawing in the museum was amazing work for a child who had scored at the 8th percentile on pencil/paper tests and

Figure 5.
Scott's Sketches from a Visit
to the Seattle Art Museum

who had in several previous years received N's (needs improve-
ment) in working independently and small-muscle control. In the
context of our classroom, where multiple sign systems and inquiry
counted, he could safely develop along his own pathway and at a
pace more accommodating of his abilities and talents.

The more the invitations I created reflected Scott's interests,
the more I was able to see what he was capable of achieving. For
example, he was very interested in the slinky and could arrange
stacks of blocks so that its route was direct and quick—arranging
and rearranging the blocks and the distance between them, changing

the variables. I wondered, in fact, how much of his learning I could actually recognize. I wished for a physicist to work alongside, to name the principles Scott was working out.

At the end of second grade, Scott was more expressive in print, as shown in Figure 6, a typical journal entry.

He continued to sketch jets on a weekly basis and respond with art in other areas of the curriculum. His personal inquiry had also evolved, shifting from jets to weapons that Indians use to eagles

Figure 6.
A Sample of Scott's Writing at the End of Second Grade

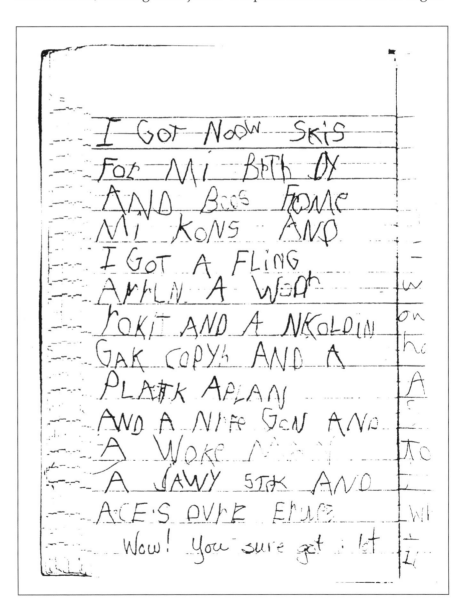

and other birds of prey. His questions focused on how eagles could swoop down so quickly—*why don't their wings just come out of the sockets?* He knew that their bone structure consisted of hollow, fingernail-like material. He had accumulated a wealth of information.

Scott's reading also sounded different. He continued to select nonfiction books during most of his choice reading times and was now dipping into the texts more extensively. During his inquiry presentations, he often showed illustrations from these books, and over time he was reading more of the text aloud. The video onto which we'd taped his series of presentations confirmed my impressions. In April, he read to us from a book on birds of prey:

Some eagles (let) other birds do their hunting for *"What does this spell?"* them. They wait until pelicans, herons, or other [pal-cons] [hérons] [their] birds make a catch—and then steal the catch [for them] from them. Here an African fish eagle is about to pounce on a pelican. In order to escape, the pelican will drop the food from its mouth.

"Some eagles . . . l-e-t . . . what does this spell? Some eagles . . . other birds do their hunting for them. They wait until palcons (he's trying to read falcons for pelicans) or her-ons (again) or their birds make their catch for them." At this point, he broke away from the text and completed his description without it, using his arms to demonstrate the scene he was sharing. This and similar readings helped me see that his reading was clearly more sophisticated than what it had been at the beginning of the year.

I could see many of Scott's strengths, yet I was also uncertain about how he would do in a third-grade classroom. If I viewed Scott as he performed on traditional school tasks, he was clearly "at risk." With his parents' endorsement, we decided he would stay with his classmates another year. He became one of four third graders in what evolved from a first- and second- to a first-, second-, and third-grade multiage classroom.

Scott through His Classmates' Eyes

Scott began the next year as a much more confident learner. I found ways to highlight the strengths of the third graders, and Scott's classmates often sought him out as a partner. However, I still had much to learn. As we approached the fall reporting period, I asked the students to share their knowledge and impressions of their classmates. I issued a single sheet of paper with each person's name written in a small box. I then asked the students to write something about each classmate—an interest, a talent, something they noticed. The next day, the names were cut apart and the students delivered their thoughts to the other kids. As shown by the various comments in Figure 7, Scott stood out in new ways once again.

Our classroom community held him in high esteem. I hadn't really known, for instance, how strong he was on the playground or

Figure 7.
Impressions of Scott as Seen through the Eyes of His Classmates

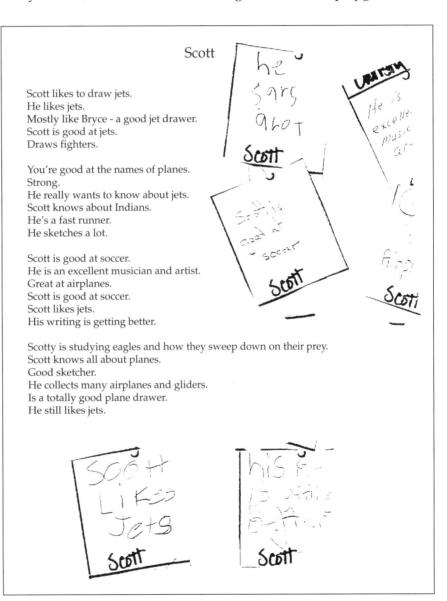

Scott likes to draw jets.
He likes jets.
Mostly like Bryce - a good jet drawer.
Scott is good at jets.
Draws fighters.

You're good at the names of planes.
Strong.
He really wants to know about jets.
Scott knows about Indians.
He's a fast runner.
He sketches a lot.

Scott is good at soccer.
He is an excellent musician and artist.
Great at airplanes.
Scott is good at soccer.
Scott likes jets.
His writing is getting better.

Scotty is studying eagles and how they sweep down on their prey.
Scott knows all about planes.
Good sketcher.
He collects many airplanes and gliders.
Is a totally good plane drawer.
He still likes jets.

that he was a capable athlete as well. I once again interviewed Scott using the Burke Reading Interview. Here, I could see significant growth in the strategies he could articulate. His view of reading, for example, was also much more complex than a year earlier.

Burke's Reading Interview
Scott O'Farrell

November 1993	**November 1994**
What is reading? (What do you think readers do?) *They look at words. I like airplanes. I have airplane books.*	What do you think reading is? *It's something you can do, 'cause it's kinda fun reading books.*
When you are reading and you come to something you don't know, what do you do? *I try to ... I ask my friends. Also, if they didn't know, I would try to sound it out or if they didn't know, ask another friend.*	When you are reading and you come to something you don't know, what do you do? *I try to look at the pictures. I sound it out slowly— try to get a word that's close to it. I know what the book is about so I can figure it out that way maybe. I try different sounds or sometimes I skip it.*
Who is a good reader you know? What makes him a good reader? *Nicholas, because we like to buddy read and I help him read words if he can't figure them out.*	Who is a good reader you know? What makes him a good reader? *Bryce, because he kind of practices more than me. Well, me and my grandpa are building a model and he helps me read some of the words because I told him I'm not that good yet. I'm not that good, like the best in the classroom and I'm a third grader so I should be. My reading is like 2nd grade level.*
Do you suppose Nicholas ever comes to anything he doesn't know? What do you think he does? *Yes, he asks me and I try to help him. He might ask another friend.*	Do you suppose Bryce ever comes to anything he doesn't know? What do you think he does? *Not very much I don't think ... well my mom had trouble too—with the longest word there is—because it didn't make much sense. It didn't have many spaces.*
If you knew someone was having trouble reading, how would you help that person? *Try to sound it out for them.*	If you knew someone was having trouble reading, how would you help that person? *They might just skip it if they just can't sound it out.*

What would a teacher do to help that person?
Might ask them to read it if they didn't know what t-h-e spelled.

What would a teacher do to help that person?
They would help sound it out, like what sound does this make or this is silent so don't count that or say try hard to think about it.

How did you learn to read?
In first grade I learned some sounds and letters like the and to; sounding letters out.

How did you learn to read?
In my old class we made little books like Pat and cat sit on hat—little rhyming books pretty much.

What would you like to do better as a reader?
Get a different book.

What would you like to do better as a reader?
I want to learn like bigger words—like when my mom reads books like The Bismark. I already know how to read that because we've read it two times. Once my mom reads it then I know it a pretty long time.

Do you think you are a good reader? Why?
Yeah, pretty good.

Do you think you are a good reader? Why?
I'm an okay reader—not really good. But I'm better than some of the first graders. And once my friend got stuck and I knew the word and he even reads chapter books and I've only read one chapter book.

How could we help you at school?
Help me sound out words better.

How could we help you at school?
I don't know. I'm not sure. My mom doesn't tell me every word, or I won't be able to read when I grow up. Some adults never did learn how to read; they're like too poor to go to school or something.

How could your parents help you at home?
My mom tells me "what does this say?" like on some street signs.

How could your parents help you at home?
I'm not sure. My mom reads to me most every night unless we get home late.

Nonetheless, his written work still indicated a child "at risk." I certainly felt anxious when he didn't express his ideas more fully in writing. When I asked him to respond, after an invitation time, to "what did you do?" he wrote, I MAD the SLINGKY GO DOWN THE WOD Steþs (Figure 8).

Figure 8.
Scott's Written Work
That Shows Him to Be an
"At-Risk" Child

Not only were his ideas incomplete but also his spelling didn't reflect information he knew. In this example, he omits punctuation and the silent /e/ that had been the focus of spelling strategy lessons. Similarly, when we were involved in a "book buddy letter" homework project (the students were asked to read a book each week and write a letter to a buddy describing the book—an activity that offered a chance to focus on editing strategies at home with parents), Scott's mom was challenged to get him moving on the assignment. He remarked, in an Eeyore kind of voice, "Why do I have to write to him? He's in my class—I could just tell him." What seemed to others minimal effort often became on Scott's part a pragmatic and practical stance from his point of view.

Scott through His Own Eyes

It was at this time—after a year of working with Scott—that I accepted an invitation to speak at an NCTE session with Linda Crafton on "assessment as inquiry." A short time into the planning I realized that I wasn't quite sure what the term meant. I was documenting student learning in new ways and believed that the narrative reports we wrote were doing a better job of capturing Scott's development than the report cards from his kindergarten and first-grade experiences. In kindergarten he received N's in several areas: listens attentively and follows through, follows directions, works carefully, works independently, participates in group discussions, and small muscle control. He received N's also in scissors, pencils, paint, and drawing. The only written comment said, "Scott seems very slow and methodical." In first grade the report was a series of X's, slashes, and blank boxes along with the comments: "Scott has a very inquisitive mind and I enjoy having him in class. Scott's learning more words will help his reading success. Have a great summer."

I wondered what his parents thought? Although they could clearly see his struggles with reading, writing, and math, they received little sense of what he looked like as a learner at school. Therefore, in the narrative reports I wrote, I endeavored to describe Scott's learning in more specific ways. For instance, I wrote about his reading in terms of specific books and strategies, changes in his attitude, and how his work at home was helping toward his improvements at school. Locating his abilities along a reading continuum helped us value where he'd been and where he was headed, albeit behind many of his peers.

As I explained the narrative reports to Linda, I told her that I felt I was creating better opportunities to see Scott as a learner. She gently pushed me, "Now Kathy, do you think the issue is that you create better opportunities to see who Scott is or that you talk to Scott about his views of his learning?" Although I found both perspectives to be important ones, Linda's push impelled me to spend more time listening to Scott's ideas about himself as a learner. Clearly, Linda was urging me to more actively pull Scott into the assessment process.

I had solicited ideas from Scott and conducted reading interviews with him, but when I returned to talk with him again, I did so in an entirely new way. I wanted to capture his view of himself, so I listened to his ideas and interests and then set out to photograph him doing the things he mentioned. I put together a report, "Scott as a Learner," that included photographs of him at work doing the things he valued. I began each section of the report with his own written words and added comments he told me in further questioning. (Part of this report is published in the *Standards in Practice, Grades K–2*, NCTE, 1996). When I went to NCTE in March 1996 to present, there was no doubt I knew Scott in ways in which I hadn't known him before.

As I later read across each of the reports I'd written about Scott in the previous two years, and then I read the one I'd composed with Scott's views and language, I recognized my perspective as just one small piece, or commentary, in the total picture of who Scott is as a learner. Further, I understand the necessity of keeping the questions I offered to frame his ideas open to questioning and revision—so that the reporting isn't dominated or overwhelmed by my perspective. Authentic assessment requires an inquiry perspective.

Figure 9.
Two Pages from My Report
"Scott as a Learner" (from
*Standards in Practice,
Grades K–2,* NCTE)

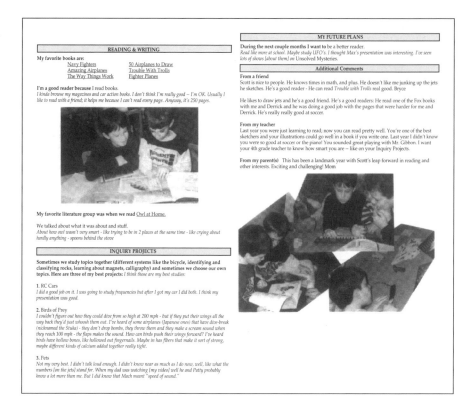

Scott went on to fourth grade and we keep in touch. He is a confident reader and confided that he's worked hard on his handwriting because he doesn't want his friends to think he's "dumb." His writing has also improved immensely: for example, he develops ideas more fully, he more readily takes up topics beyond his immediate interests, and he more willingly edits and revises. His reading plays an active role in his thinking as a writer. He has found ways to explore his interests through "math investigations," as well as the ongoing inquiry projects that help shape the curriculum.

As I consider Scott and the role our classroom environment played in his early education, I feel confident we rescued him from years of the remedial treatment he'd experienced as a first grader. My classroom was not a showy space, with few fancy bulletin boards, few electronic gadgets. Rather, a new understanding of learning—broader, more encompassing of the whole child—helped me to create an environment where Scott could make connections in ways that made sense to him. Within that supportive context I could push him—but not so far that he was off balance. I then made it my job, and his, to describe the learning that occurred. Together, Scott and I learned to value his strengths. Together, we developed a more competent learner and more confident person.

Nathaniel

Barry T. Hoonan

Nathaniel came along at a time when I was struggling with my own understanding of how the arts relate to learning. In my fifth-/sixth-grade classroom, I had always made writing a priority. The students routinely wrote in learning logs and journals to capture what they felt, comprehended, and learned while researching. We used a message board and mailboxes for personal communications. We also published a monthly magazine. Writing comprised a major part of the curriculum, providing me with a means to evaluate students and providing the students with the means to inform me about what they knew.

Questioning My Curriculum

Having read *Frames of Mind: The Theory of Multiple Intelligences* by Howard Gardner (1983), I was beginning to question the prominent role verbal and mathematical thinking played in my curriculum. Gardner's work convinced me there were multiple intelligences, and I was determined to incorporate more art, drama, and music experiences into my teaching. I began to invite children to use art and drama to respond to literature and to reflect on experiences. The students liked these invitations, and I was pleased to think I had discovered some new ways to get them to enjoy reading and writing.

I had decided to be more systematic about including the arts, so I began planning an integrated unit about immigration and its history in the USA. I was trying to think of ways I could integrate more art experiences with the curriculum's critical content. I shared my ideas with Kathy Egawa, and she challenged my assumption that teaching with the arts meant adding art experiences onto what I already did. She suggested that I think about what it means to make sense of the world through art and that I "live" an experience with some artists.

I felt uneasy with the subtleties of all this. I mean, what's the difference between thinking of art as something your class does to enhance learning and thinking of art itself as learning? Our conversations and the challenge of this question led me to invite a poet, a dancer, a graphic artist, and a chef to my house for dinner. I read two children's books to this group: *Polly Vaughan*, a dark and tragic Appalachian Romeo and Juliet tale, written and illustrated by Barry Moser, and *Fly Away Home*, a story written by Eve Bunting about a homeless family who lives at the airport. First, we discussed the books, and then I suggested we meet again in a week, prepared with a response to one of the two books.

The chef asked, "How many pages do you want me to write?" I replied that I hoped each artist could find a relationship to the book through their skilled way of knowing. The artist looked at me quizzically, and the dancer asked again what I meant. I suggested that she consider thinking about responding to one of the books through dance. "Do I need to say anything? Write anything?" she asked.

"No," I said. "It would be fine were you to dance your response. In fact, I am hoping each of you will express your response in a manner that fits your particular artistic way of thinking."

Our next meeting began with the dancer. She had choreographed a four-minute dance to Annie Lennox's song "Little Bird." Her choreography suggested the constrained steps of a "not to be noticed" boy who moved toward a light, which appeared hopeful and blossoming. We chatted for several minutes about what her dance meant to us and what connections it brought out that we originally had not noticed in the book. We were hooked. For the next hour, the five of us were entirely engaged. The artist brought out a metaphorical comparison between flight and hope, complicated by money. The chef offered a sirloin roast tied up in a dirty rope, served on a rusty tin, and the poet read a piece she had written about her neighbor who shared much in common with the boy in *Fly Away Home*. The artifacts they had created generated many new insights about the books and about our own lives and stories.

New Sign Systems, New Possibilities

As Kathy had predicted, this experience changed me. I acquired a different sense of what was possible when learners used various sign systems to make meaning. I started to wonder how this experience could and should change things in my classroom. I thought a lot about how I used art in relation to literature extensions. We read books together, often wrote responses, and explored new interpretations and new insights through drama, drawing, collage, music, and poetry. I valued all these extension activities, although I focused on literature. Even though dance, painting, and collage work might be going on in my class, if students were not reading lots of books, I worried. If students were not writing for our class magazine, *Why Not?* I was concerned.

Nathaniel

The main lens I used for looking at learners was a very conventional one, based on the belief that literacy involves only reading and writing. For this reason, Nathaniel was causing me real concern. By fall conference time, he had not finished a single book, and his participation in literature circles created a problem. The members in his literature groups complained that he wasn't reading the pages assigned and that he was coming unprepared. He often tried to read the book during the discussions instead of listening to the conversation. Eventually, his classmates excluded him from literature circles, and even this act did not motivate Nathaniel to keep up with the assigned reading. He had failed to participate successfully with two different groups, and he seemed not to care that he was an outsider in class.

In addition, Nathaniel had escaped all my attempts to get him to write for the class magazine. As far as I could tell, the first two months of school had been wasted with Nathaniel. He was unengaged as a reader or writer, and I believed he was learning very little.

Nathaniel was thin and very tall for a fifth grader, standing just two inches short of six feet. When he arrived with his parents for his conference and I watched him slide into place beside them, I wondered whether his size contributed some part to his having such a difficult time fitting in. Searching for somewhere to begin, I pulled out Nathaniel's reading list. He had nothing recorded, so I asked Nathaniel if he liked reading and he responded, "Sure. I just don't do it very often. Mostly, I do it in class when I'm not talking to someone."

We discussed the difficulties Nathaniel was having in class, how he had yet to contribute to the class magazine, and how the other students felt justified in excluding him from their conversations. I wanted to convey the seriousness of the situation, but I did not get much sense that Nathaniel saw anything wrong with his performance. Finally, I decided the hole was deep enough and we should move on to something else.

As a rule, I ask my students to complete 240 minutes of homework each week, and I expect them to use this time to engage in inquiry about topics of their own interest. I asked Nathaniel what he was working on at home. At this point in the conference I was feeling frustrated and less than hopeful. In class, the students and I often talked about possibilities for this individual work, and they frequently shared how they were spending their time. Oddly enough, I realized at this moment, I had never heard a word from Nathaniel about the work he was doing.

Nathaniel's mom suddenly grew more animated. "Nathaniel, have you ever shown Mr. Hoonan your designs of stuff you do at home?"

As the conference continued, I found out that Nathaniel designed and built tree houses. In fact, building tree houses was his passion, an interest that had overflowed into house and boat designs as well. He was using archaic computer software to draw these designs in the beginning but had since discovered his neighbors' sophisticated computer system, which would let him do architectural drawings. I heard myself saying, "Okay Nathaniel, you haven't finished a piece of writing yet this year. You haven't completed a book. Why don't you write about what you enjoy, like designing."

In retrospect, I wish I had encouraged Nathaniel to write about his interest because I recognized that he was learning through drawing and that he had a passion and an interest in design (Figures 1a and 1b).

Figures 1a and 1b.
Nathaniel's Designs of Tree Houses Using Computer Software

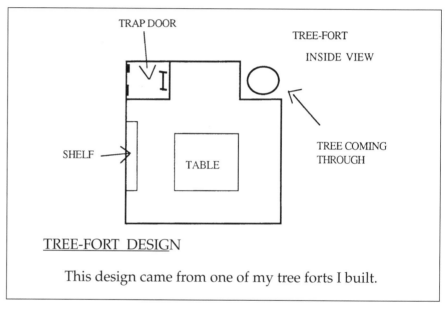

TRAP DOOR

TREE-FORT

INSIDE VIEW

SHELF

TABLE

TREE COMING
THROUGH

TREE-FORT DESIGN

This design came from one of my tree forts I built.

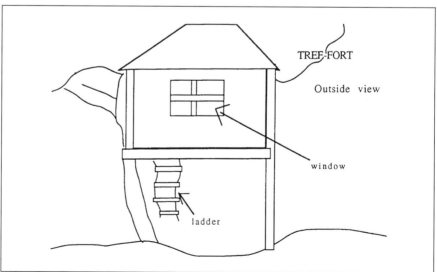

TREE-FORT

Outside view

window

ladder

Truthfully, I wanted him to write because I could not let go of my old frame of reference. Even though I was beginning to realize that people could make meaning in sign systems other than language, published writing still counted most in my mind. I valued the writing he did for the class magazine more than his portfolio of drawings. I saw drawing as an enhancement to writing, not as a means for thinking and learning. When Nathaniel produced this first draft of writing about the design work, I finally breathed a little easier (Figure 2). He was writing. He was learning.

Although I was pleased when Nathaniel was published in our class magazine, I was uneasy in my pleasure. I kept thinking about Nathaniel's extraordinary gift for drawing and about how much I had learned about him by talking to his parents. Was my focus on reading and writing getting in Nathaniel's way—impeding his progress in some manner? I began to wonder what else I was missing. How would different options in the class for Nathaniel and others like him show what they knew?

Figure 2.
A Sample of
Nathaniel's Writing

BY: Nathaniel Erman

I like designing because it makes me feel like i'm inside the structure I'm designing. I've designed lots of things, houses, mansions, airplanes, boats, space ships and treeforts. I also have drawn maps of places, like towns & forests. I design whenever I have freetime. The biggest thing I ever designed (and the first thing i rely ever designed) was a mansion that every relitive of mine I could think lived in. It added up to about 73 people.

Imostly design mansions. I like to pretend I live in the mansions. I first got started in designing when I tried to draw a house with my cousin, Jonny Talbott. Here are some designs I have made and with each design I've included some descriptions and why I like the design.

Inquiry and Multiple Ways of Knowing

This uncertainty led me back to Kathy Egawa's door. Like me, she had students who were making little traditional progress, and she suggested we each study one of these children. She was convinced that we needed to watch these students through a different lens, through inquiry and multiple ways of knowing, and that we needed to make sure we were teaching in ways that made inquiry and multiple ways of knowing part of the curriculum. She talked to me about the inquiry cycle and "expert studies"—learners choosing for themselves the kinds of things they wanted to study and teachers providing strategies, time, and support for their deep inquiries. While I was allowing this kind of work to happen at home, I was not honoring it in the classroom. Kathy agreed to support me as I made this transition.

In January, Kathy and I found an opportunity to build expert studies into the established curriculum. The school PTSA sponsored a space project and hired a retired scientist/engineer from NASA to turn our school into a "self-sufficient moon base" called Moon Base Alpha. Each section of our building was given different responsibilities, and the scientist provided the experiments we needed to help the children learn key concepts of weightlessness, gravity, space travel, and plant care. Although the curriculum for the project was set, Kathy and I decided to go beyond the planned events. We began by asking our students what they personally wanted to learn about the moon base. This probe to explore individually further led students to pose their own questions, conduct their own research, and, finally, present their observations and conclusions in a presentation before their peers.

Nathaniel, normally reticent about work, found the invitation to list his own questions and learn about space and the moon motivating. His energy and enthusiasm surprised me. When it came to reading at school, Nathaniel generally displayed disinterest and saw himself as playing a small, if any, role in the curriculum. With expert studies, however, he eagerly engaged in reading, talking, note taking, and sketching—through curiosity and sheer captivation. Expert studies captured his personal desire to know, question, and investigate.

In his expert studies journal, Nathaniel sketched, doodled, and noted details that he found interesting about the moon and earth. He noted, *"Some scientists believe the moon is a chunk out of the earth because there is a big deep spot the size of the moon in the Pacific Ocean."* The questions in his journal reflected his wonder about size and relationships. He queried, *"If the earth was the size of a basketball, wouldn't the moon be about the size of a tennis ball?"* His journal not only highlighted data and questions he was collecting but also revealed what he thought was important. Nathaniel seemed to be consumed with the matter of who should live on the base. He scribbled out reasons for why scientists, gym teachers, actors, and "fix-it" men should be sent there.

As the culminating project, each student would share a five- to ten-minute presentation resulting from personal inquiry. Nathaniel's interest and skill in design came into full view again as he decided to create a design for Moon Base Alpha. He teamed up with Evan—a sixth-grade classmate who also had difficulty completing projects—and together they developed a rather thorough model, as shown in Figure 3.

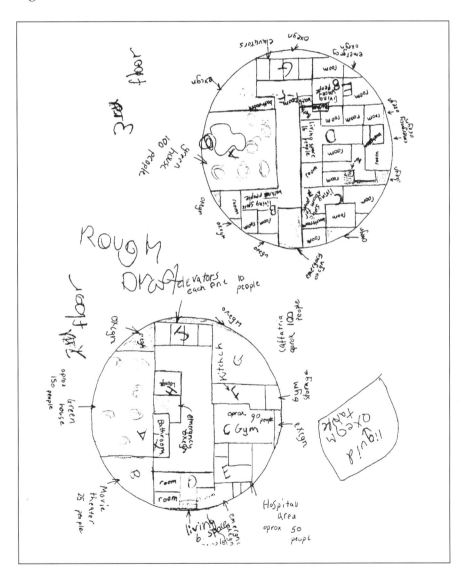

Figure 3.
Nathaniel's Design for
Moon Base Alpha

During their class presentation, Nathaniel and Evan explained the compartmentalized oxygen rooms and the recreation area. Everything was designed to scale and to a certain set of specifications. Nathaniel revealed that the design, the writing on the side of the plans, and most of the ideas were his. When asked about Evan's contribution, Evan interjected, "I kept Nathaniel focused."

Nathaniel and Evan's plan was displayed on the class bulletin board alongside other drawings, models, and writing. One day I was studying this board carefully while waiting for my class, and I realized that the boys had accomplished an impressive amount of writing in a relatively short amount of time. I also realized, in that moment, that I had come to favor the class magazine to the exclusion of all other kinds of writing and expression. I had decided whether a child was successful in our class by the amount of writing he or she contributed to the magazine. Our grading conversations in the class centered on the published pieces in the magazine. The moon base on the wall, filled with visual and written content, couldn't be reduced. It was not going to be in our magazine, but it was worth valuing.

With Nathaniel's moon base design lingering in my mind, I went back to his portfolio. I skipped through some reading responses I had marked earlier in the year, and two unnoticed papers surfaced. The first was Nathaniel's visual response to *The Secret Garden.* While I had given him feedback about his written response, I had made no comment about his intricate drawing of the garden in the book (Figure 4). Had I failed to see it or failed to find importance in it? The other response was one Nathaniel had written about Stephen Biesty's picture book *Cross-sections Man-of-War.* Who else but a passionate designer and builder would love a book filled with detailed drawings of a fighting ship?

It dawned on me that Nathaniel was trying to find his way into the curriculum, but I was oblivious to his attempts. While his illustrated responses were impressive and fascinating, I didn't place much value on them because they were not written. And, because I held literature and other fiction works in high esteem, I tended to gloss over Nathaniel's reviews of nonfiction books. Nathaniel's enthusiasm for expert studies, though, was helping me understand that most students try to fit into the curriculum in the best way they know how. They each bring some talent or acumen to the classroom that may or may not be readily recognizable, and it's important that I acknowledge their personal ways of knowing.

Nathaniel taught me to think beyond the classroom and to look for the ways in which knowing and learning evolved from every context in life. To know him as a learner, I needed to know that he loved baseball. I also needed to know that his body was not cooperating with his passion for the game. Admittedly, I did not put

Figure 4.
Nathaniel's Drawing
of a Garden Showing
Intricate Detail

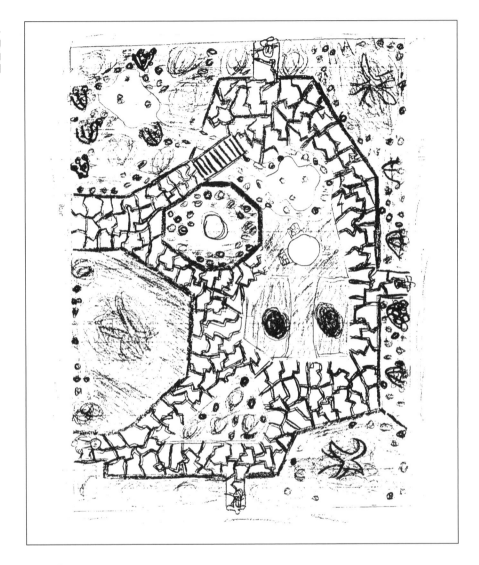

all this together until Nathaniel wrote his second contribution—a
personal narrative about a baseball accident—to our class magazine.
He arduously began sketching the details of the story on paper and
was later supported in writing the piece by student editors and by
our class editor, Pam Goodfellow of Goodfellow Press.

Nathaniel's story caused me to reflect on the beginning of the
school year. Nathaniel would sprint out to the baseball field every
recess, but he was always the last to be picked for a team. In fact, at
one point, second graders were being chosen before Nathaniel, who
had difficulty coordinating his tall, growing body. Also, Nathaniel
could not hit the ball, and for this his teammates had no sympathy.

They teased and ridiculed him so badly that Nathaniel, feeling insulted and frustrated by the game he loved best, shrugged home. I had suggested that Nathaniel might make a better choice of games to play during recess, again devaluing his passions and interests. I failed to understand his love for baseball; I failed to understand Nathaniel's ways of knowing.

In March, baseball and design both returned again as Nathaniel's themes of choice. He chose to do his expert study on Ebbets Field, home of the Brooklyn Dodgers, and decided to build the inside of the park. Nathaniel read and wrote about Ebbets Field, and he delivered an oral presentation on how he learned to scale the infield and outfield measurements. He also discussed how he decided on the colors and how difficult it was to make little ball players for his diorama.

As I think back, I realize that I could have helped Nathaniel connect his own constructed knowledge to the mathematics I was trying to teach. While he was able to make a drawing to scale and explain the mathematics of the process, he was less successful at memorizing the multiplication and division facts and doing long division. Yet facts and correct answers to problems in the math book were my yardstick of success. I was busy checking off these skills in the students' portfolios, but ignoring the math in the students' projects. Lucky for me—and for him—Nathaniel did not shut down. Even though I failed to acknowledge his successful use of math in such projects, being able to design and draw gave Nathaniel a space wherein he felt successful. His peers appreciated his work, and he was gaining stature in their eyes. Based on my evaluations, he was saying, "I'm lousy at math. I don't know all my multiplication and division facts. I can add and subtract pretty good, but when it comes to long division . . . forget it! I'm bad." In spite of this proclamation, he was developing credibility with his classmates who saw him as a serious learner.

In the spring, I took my class on a nature walk outside our school. A red-tailed hawk flew over, and I just happened to be alongside Nathaniel. He began to recite a long list of facts about red-tailed hawks. He talked for four or five minutes to me and other students who gathered near. He told us he had been observing hawks for a long time in his backyard.

Later that week I informed the students that it was time to choose their topic for another expert study. Nathaniel's response was typical. "I don't know what to do." As I thought about the students and the choices they were making, I wondered about Nathaniel. Why did he struggle so with coming up with an expert study topic when he obviously had deep interest in certain things, the red-tailed hawk, for example? He had never mentioned this interest until we were outside. Yet he spoke so eloquently and passionately from his own experiences that the other students wanted to listen to him.

I suggested to Nathaniel that learning more about hawks would be perfect for his next expert study. He agreed. I thought that Nathaniel would write like he spoke about hawks, that he would passionately tell about the birds he knew from years of observation. I thought he would use his artistic way of knowing to illustrate his favorite observations and stories. Instead, he turned to the electronic encyclopedia and collected facts. He wrote a five-paragraph report that parroted the print resource (Figure 5). Then he announced that he was done.

I realize now that I missed the chance to have an important conversation with Nathaniel. Somehow, choosing a topic of interest to him did not bridge the world of school and the world of his own experiences. None of his own observations, nor his way of seeing birds in his own world, made it into the project. While he was acting like a scientist in his own environment, at school he was "academic"—keeping his distance and remaining uninvolved personally. I would later discover the point of his hesitation to be more personally involved.

Spring had arrived and renewed our energy, providing us with fresh momentum. The students were beginning to find writing increasingly easier, so I assigned another report. Nathaniel spun back to baseball to fulfill the writing requirement. As I was looking over his baseball inquiry, I realized he had some pretty powerful questions. It was not just how big Ebbets Field was. It was Who invented the game? Why had it become so popular? What different baseball places could he visit if he had the money? Nathaniel could carry on an interesting conversation about baseball, which, although I appreciated, I failed to recognize the perseverance this represented. He chose his baseball report to put into his portfolio and wrote this reflection about why he made that choice (Figure 6).

Nathaniel had never given up on baseball. He just dug in deeper, and he was beginning to see a connection between what he was learning in school and his own interests and endeavors. Perhaps this insight set the stage for the incredible breakthrough that followed. It was spring parent conference time, and I was concerned this time for another boy in my class, Ryan. Although Ryan was writing a lot, he just did not do much polishing for publication. Simply, Ryan enjoyed writing, but he was not very invested in going through the required revising and editing stages.

At Ryan's conference, with him and his mother in attendance, I drew on what I had learned from Nathaniel's conference. I asked about what Ryan loved to do. His mom mentioned that he often rewrote sports stories at home. In fact, he had just completed a two-

Figure 5.
Nathaniel's Five-Paragraph
Essay about Hawks

By Nathaniel Erman

FOOD

Hawks are beautful birds; and well fitted meat eaters. Hawks prey on Rabbit, Mice, Snakes and bacicaly any animals that are smaller than a rabbit. Hawks use thier sharp claws to siese animals, and thier rasor like bill to tear of flesh. They do not eat bugs because they are to big to catch enugh to live on. Hawks are known for chickens from time to time. They do there hunting during the day only. Hawks and thier relitives help farmers grately by killing animals that harm or eat crops. hawks capture liveing animals and killthem instantly for food. They swallow prey hole. Matieral that canot be destinggished is thrown up in pellets. Hawks eat bones, feathers, and fur as well as flesh. Hawks play an important role in the balance of nature by preying on such small animals as mice, and rats. There is probaly no animals that hawks

THE BODY

A hawks eyes are one of it's most important parts of it's outside body. The hawk sees less with both eyes than with each eye seperatly. From a distance a human see's a rabbit as a blur but a hawk see's it clearly . The two fields of visionoverlap in a small area. They have sharp eye sight about 8 times as sharp as a human bieng's.
They have good strong beaks for tearing meat. They have strong wings that are good for swooping down, fast on prey. They have strong feet for grabing and carring away prey. Male hawks range from 10-22 inches in length, and the females from 12-26 inches in length. The female hawk is usaly stronger, largrer, and bolder than the male. Thier wings are slightly rounder and broader than the falcon's(a fellow bird of prey). Most hawks have light colored eyes which give them a fierce look. They do not sing but when bothered they utter a piercing whistle along with scream's and chattering call's.

HOME LIFE

Hawks seldomo meet in groups of three or more exept during migration periods. The male and female uasaly prefer to make thier nest alone, and they defend their privacy from other hawks, as well as from large birds, animals and people. Some of the larger hawks have attacked people who came to close too their nests, causing painful cuts with thier sharp talons. The male helps hatch the egg's and care for the young. Hawks usually use the same nest year after year. Most hawks build thier nest's in high trees. Others build them in bushes, on cliffs or on the ground. The female lays two to six eggs depending about what kind of hawk. The eggs hatch after 3-4 weeks. Larger hawks take the longest to hatch. At first the young hawks are covered with a whitish down and are quite helpless . The parents bring food to the nest, tear it open and drop it in the eager, open mouths. As the young grow older they lose they lose thier down and grow feathers, a little duller in coler than those of it's parent's. They fly from the nest after a month or six weeks.

RELITIVES

The relitives of the hawk are all daytime birds of prey (except some owls) and meat- eaters they are the condor, falcon, ospry, and secratary bird familys.

Figure 5.
Continued

ENIMIES

Natruly human biengs are a big threat an danger to hawks with dangerous poisons and sport hunting. But ravens (crows) are the real enemy. For example, say a hawk gliding around looking for prey, if a group of crows are come by they will dive at the hawk, attack, and pecked at it. (crows uasaly attack at smaller hawks) With this happening the hawk is helpless, the hawk is not enough for a bunch of crows. So the hawk will fly to the closest and will be protected by the branches of the tree.

Figure 6.
Nathaniel's Report
on Baseball

BASEBALL REPORT

I chose my baseball report because it was the Expert Studies Project that I had the most fun with. I learned so much about the game of baseball it even helped me improve my playing.

---

page piece about Nancy Kerrigan. Ryan's mother turned to him and asked why he had not shared it. Typically, he replied, "I don't know." I asked Ryan if he would be interested in creating his own sports magazine at school. Ryan walked away from the conference the new editor of a sports magazine for kids.

On Monday Ryan announced to the class that he was creating a new sports magazine. He instructed all interested classmates to meet at his table during writing time. Seven children huddled around Ryan's table that morning, and they decided that the *Real Side of Sports* would be a weekly magazine. The first deadline would be Wednesday, just two days away. Nathaniel was invited into this magazine group because his classmates had noticed that he drew very well (Figure 7). He was assigned the role of sports artist.

I was watching this *Real Side of Sports* group with great interest because they had given themselves one week to publish, when our class magazine, *Why Not?* usually took about six weeks to be delivered. I was also well aware that all the contributors were boys, several of whom had been guided, pushed, and supported by every living resource in the class to complete previous pieces of writing. By Wednesday, Nathaniel and Ryan were spending their lunch period typing articles. Nathaniel contributed his typing, his art work, and even his own writing. This was a breakthrough considering that all year he had contributed only two pieces to *Why Not?* Now, in the course of three days, he had completely immersed

Figure 7.
Nathaniel's Illustration for
the *Real Side of Sports*

himself in this sports writing and publication. By Friday, my reluctant boy writers marched out with the first edition of the *Real Side of Sports*. There were errors, but it was a hit. Other students, Tessa, for example, an accomplished writer and editor, complimented the magazine and offered to help edit the next issue.

I was amazed. True, the magazine was filled with errors, but they published it in a week. They also managed to get a second and improved edition out the following week, and then they were done—exhausted by the hard work. Yet for Nathaniel, the sports magazine proved a turning point. Life at school had changed for the better. There were positive and powerful social relations working for him. Being liked for the things he could do well motivated him. He could draw. He could type. He was a nice kid, and his classmates liked to work with him.

The final unit of curriculum for the year was the immigration unit I had been developing with Kathy's collaboration. Our conversations about sign systems led us to write a grant to fund the support of a visual artist and dancer. We invited these specialists to help us explore the concept of immigration. With the artist, our classes focused on icons, and we made hats with symbols representing the things we most valued and would take with us were we suddenly uprooted from our homes. Nathaniel placed a picture of himself in his hat in his portfolio and wrote, "I chose my icon hat because it was a lot of fun to make and it is a lot of fun to wear. I also chose my hat because it represents immigration."

I remember reading Nathaniel's reflection about the hat soon after our experience with the dancer. Kathy and I struggled some with the dancer who was not accustomed to using dance the way we envisioned using it. We asked him to help us plan activities that would enable our students to explore the meaning of immigration, to *think* through dance. He was concerned that the students begin learning about movement through learning dance skills—the system of dance. After further discussion with him, we realized we wanted to accomplish both.

When the dancer arrived, we gathered in the gym and warmed up by following his moves. Next, we began to invent moves of our own based on the stories and images of immigration that now filled our memories. I was participating in this impromptu dance, so I was not totally focused on the children, but I did notice Nathaniel's total involvement. He was sliding, swaying, and wriggling on the floor, his lanky body totally absorbed in the movement. He was very enthusiastic about the dance experience. When I asked the kids if we should have Jack, the dancer, back, he was the first to raise his hand and exclaim, "Yeah, that was really great!" Later, as I looked at photos Kathy and I took during the activity, I realized that Nathaniel was in heaven during this experience. His smile told the whole story.

When I read Nathaniel's hat reflection, stating that his hat represented immigration, I laughed to myself. Nathaniel knew what I was working so hard to learn myself. There are many ways to represent what we know. For Nathaniel, written language and school mathematics were a stretch. He often was out of his comfort zone. He connected best when he was using art or movement to know the world. And he persisted in following his own path, trusting his own questions in spite of his lack of success along more conventional pathways.

Reflections on My Teaching and Learning

As I reflect on Nathaniel's learning experiences in my classroom, I have some regrets. Even though I was beginning to understand that all sign systems are powerful and can be used to make meaning, I prioritized reading and writing and school mathematics. I needed this experience of seeing a child through a lens colored by inquiry and multiple ways of knowing. It changed what I know to look for and what I see. In retrospect, I see that Nathaniel was learning in ways that go beyond what we typically value in school and that he had the courage to sustain his personal inquiries in spite of the messages he received telling him he was a poor learner. I see places in the relationship between the two of us where I could have helped him build a bridge between ways of knowing and more traditional school criteria. I can better see that Nathaniel's body played a huge role in his learning and that, except on one occasion, I neglected that discovery in the classroom.

The good news is that Nathaniel is okay. In sixth grade, he went on to develop more sophistication as a reader and a writer and more confidence as a social participant in the classroom. The connections between home and school improved, and Nathaniel, with the help of his parents, took on the task of designing and building an outdoor amphitheater for the class.

I am changed for the good as well. In part, I have learned the power of belonging to an inquiry community. I did not make this journey alone; but rather, I made it with many traveling companions who listened while I formulated my thoughts and who challenged me to think again from different perspectives. As I worked to understand Nathaniel through the questions he pursued and sign systems he used, I learned to see a learner in ways that before were only peripheral for me. I discovered how to step back and bring into focus the larger picture when thinking about a learner. It follows that I can now better know and support individual learners. These experiences have rewarded me by helping me develop into a better teacher, into a teacher who can more fully understand how to engage the individual learner.

From Theory to Practice

Beth Berghoff

Model of Curriculum based
on Inquiry and Multiple
Ways of Knowing

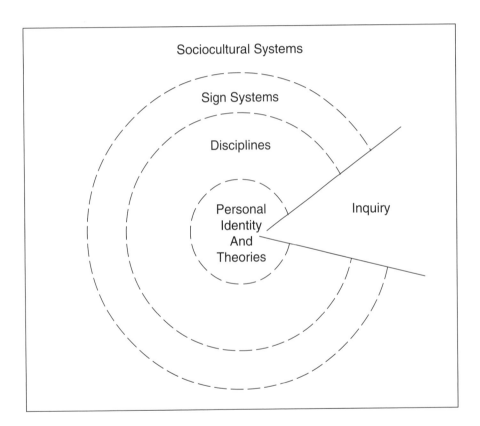

This simple model represents fundamental changes in the way we as teachers understand learners and knowledge and our relationship to them. Our efforts to translate this model into practice have taught us to think of learners as people who construct personal identities and personal theories of the world through chance experiences as well as deliberate inquiry. This subtle but important belief about learners moves us beyond thinking that we create curriculum to teach knowledge and skills. We are learning that we create curriculum to help learners change and grow as individuals, for it is the identities and theories of the learners that eventually determine what they do with the knowledge and skills that they learn in school.

This model also represents a shift toward multiple ways of knowing. In this model, disciplines are not the primary focus of curriculum, but rather are one of the three key systems used in the process of learning. Both sign systems and sociocultural systems are of parallel importance. Learners gather equally important information from each of these systems as they piece together their understanding of themselves and the world.

In previous chapters, we told individual stories of our attempts to put inquiry and multiple ways of knowing into practice as we created curriculum and attempted to profile the identity and theory development of some of our learners. We want to be a little more explicit in this final chapter about what we think we learned and how we learned it. We will focus on three different aspects of our experience. First, we will explore one of our most hopeful insights—that this theory in practice can help us as teachers and others in our learning communities to provide better support to learners who have been marginalized in our classrooms in the past. Our language-driven curricula have not served all children equally well. There have been children in our classes whose development as readers and writers has kept them from being recognized as successful learners. This theory provides us with new lenses for viewing all learners, and, in particular, it gives us a new view of the learners who learn best in modes other than language. We can see more clearly exactly how these children are learning, and we have more avenues for encouraging their development. Second, we will focus on some of the ways we have tried to expand our own notions of literacy and include multiple sign systems in curriculum. While the construct of multiple ways of knowing goes beyond sign systems, sign systems were our focus at the time of this shared inquiry. And finally, we will reflect on our attempts to learn about and through inquiry. Our experiences have convinced us that the best way to learn about inquiry is to live and breathe it. It is not a simple progression of step-by-step activities, and experience seems to be the only avenue to knowing its complexities and power.

Support for Marginalized Learners

Inquiry is like reading in that it is an "allatonce" (all at once) process. According to the psycholinguistic theory of reading (Goodman, 1996), readers synthesize information from at least three subsystems of language—the graphophonic, syntactic, and semantic systems. The reading cycle involves collecting visual information with the eyes, but the perceptions of what a reader sees on the page and the amount of visual information a reader needs are determined by his or her predictions. As a reader creates meaning, or what Goodman describes as a "parallel text,"the reader's mental schema guide the work. The reader constantly predicts what is likely to come next in the text on the basis of his or her knowledge of the patterns of written and spoken language and knowledge of the world. And at the same time, the reader samples the visual information to confirm or disconfirm these predictions.

We believe that inquiry is likewise a process of constructing meaning by synthesizing information from multiple systems—the sign, sociocultural, and knowledge systems. Inquirers constantly predict and confirm, question and experiment, collect and synthesize. Inquiry, however, is a far more complex meaning-making process than reading because the text is the whole world, everything in it and on it, everything imagined and beyond. Inquiry is a deliberate process wherein we construct internal texts that give meaning to our experiences.

When we build curriculum around inquiry, we put this active intellectual process at the center of school life. By involving learners in cycles of collaborative inquiry, we demonstrate deliberate learning. We immerse students in a series of subprocesses such as observation, conversation, dialogue, and collaborative work that build on one another and help the learners reflect on what they are coming to understand and how they are learning.

As Kathy and Barry began thinking more about the relationship between inquiry and multiple ways of knowing, they decided to watch and learn from two students who were not moving along the mainstream track in their classes. They were concerned about Scott and Nathaniel and interested in observing how these boys responded to a curriculum based on inquiry and multiple ways of knowing. In theory, Kathy and Barry believed that all learners could contribute to the social-learning process of the class, as well as advance their own learning. In actuality, however, these students were not confident learners, and Kathy and Barry were hoping to see positive results from changes they made in the curriculum.

Some of the changes Kathy and Barry made in their teaching constituted very simple ones. They started more deliberate and frequent use of strategies that supported the students in participating in the underlying process of inquiry. Strategies such as "Save the Last Word for Me" and "Say-Something" (Short, Harste &Burke, 1996) provided experiences wherein the children learned to take turns talking, to discover significant aspects of texts or artwork, to ask their own questions, and to respond to one another's ideas. They also offered the children choices, engaged them in dialogue, and listened to their questions. These changes were subtle, but important to creating a classroom where collaborative inquiry could take place.

The more noticeable changes came along with exploring sign system and inquiry cycles. Kathy experimented with including musical instruments and sketchpads as part of her curriculum, and Barry instituted "expert studies" in his classroom. They both began to see new dimensions of students' learning. They did not exactly know what sense to make of Scott's musical compositions or Nathaniel's tree-fort designs. They were uncertain whether they could trust these as quality learning engagements, but they were glad for something positive to build onto as they redirected these boys to language-based learning. It became clear that the alternative sign system opportunities opened avenues for intellectual engagement and that listening to the students' questions and encouraging them to follow their own interests helped to link learning in school to the children's interests and experiences outside school.

In this era of performance objectives and rubrics, teachers can easily think of learners as people who can or cannot perform certain skills. We are learning through our attempts to create inquiry and curriculum based on multiple ways of knowing that learning is never that simple. Knowing that a student can meet a particular academic standard does not tell us whether the student is becoming a resourceful and responsible human being. To us, it seems that curriculum is as much about relationships and the use of knowledge and power as it is about teaching or acquiring the expected knowledge and skills. Even though Scott was a less-capable reader, his peers accepted him, and he followed his own interests. Nathaniel, on the other hand, suffered from being ostracized by his peers and had to earn their respect by demonstrating that he had desirable strengths. The changes Kathy and Barry made in their curricula played a big role in the ways these boys came to think about themselves as learners in the context of school. Without the wider venue of learning engagements, these boys would not have had many opportunities to convince their peers that they were valuable members of the learning community. We believe Kathy and Barry's initial steps toward inquiry and multiple ways of knowing supported the boys in finding their own pathways and thereby allowed them to contribute to the shared learning of their class.

Of equal importance to being valued community members, these boys and the students in Beth and Sue's room had the advantage of being known in multiple dimensions by their teachers. When Kathy and Barry profiled Scott and Nathaniel, they made observations stemming from all three systems underlying inquiry—sign systems, knowledge systems, and sociocultural systems. Kathy described Scott's sign system capabilities and how they changed over time. At the beginning of second grade, Scott was doing little writing and laborious, slow reading. She noticed, however, that he deliberately used art as a means to record information and to think through problems. Since he also invented musical notation on his own, she concluded that he was clearly willing to risk invention within a sign system.

From a perspective of knowledge, Scott showed a clear preference for technical kinds of knowing. He attended to things that had power and motion—jets, weapons, and eagles in flight. He chose and best understood nonfiction texts. His interests included physics and structural mechanics, and in those realms, he could talk easily. And he knew a lot. Unfortunately, Scott lacked the same deep interest in other kinds of knowledge. Editing for spelling, handwriting, completing mathematics problems, and writing for the class newspaper were not as compelling to him as jets. Kathy continued to expose Scott to all kinds of knowledge, but she accepted and worked with his deep and abiding interests.

Kathy used the lens of the sociocultural system when she observed that Scott was like his father, who taught airplane design and maintenance. She recognized that children commonly want to be like the people they know best. Scott valued the technical language and focus on details. He came to school with high expectations for himself and worked hard. Even though his work often looked significantly different from the work of his peers, he had their esteem because he had uncommonly sophisticated knowledge. In collaboration with Scott's family, he spent an additional year in Kathy's classroom, moving on to the third grade with three other students. And Kathy admitted to worrying whether this year in a supportive environment would be enough to make up the lost ground, or whether his learning patterns would still result in the common cultural practices of testing and labeling when he went on to the fourth grade.

Clearly Kathy used the perspective of inquiry and multiple ways of knowing to see Scott in multiple dimensions, and this viewpoint gave her a better sense of his identity and theories about the world. She could respond to him in ways that showed respect for who he was and what he valued. And she could plan experiences that connected to his core and enticed him to try out new possibilities.

Barry's story of working with Nathaniel demonstrates what can happen when a teacher is willing to retheorize his work. Barry struggled throughout the school year with Nathaniel's resistance to reading and writing, but when he found time to look retrospectively at Nathaniel's learning, he realized that Nathaniel was trying to find his way into the curriculum through visual art, scale drawings, baseball, and movement. Despite Barry's focus on his writing, Nathaniel loved visual images and created them to go with every project. He liked baseball, even though he struggled with the poor coordination of his growing body. And he showed real enthusiasm for dance and movement. Barry realized as he wrote Nathaniel's story that he could have done more to support Nathaniel if he had been more open to Nathaniel's ways of knowing. There were many ways he could have linked to Nathaniel's interests to teach him mathematics or deepen his knowledge of hawks and baseball. Barry summed up his new perspective by saying, "I learned to step back and bring more into focus when thinking about a learner." Barry learned to think of teaching as inquiry and to recognize and value multiple ways of knowing.

Using the lenses of inquiry and multiple ways of knowing, Kathy and Barry could see more of the patterns in Scott's and Nathaniel's learning. The changes they instituted in their classrooms and in their ways of observing and assessing the children did not make the children suddenly more literate, but the new theory in practice did honor the boys' learning, whether it was happening at home or at school. And it is very hopeful to see teaching that is respectful of learners and honors diversity.

Expanding Our Notions of Literacy

Sit in the bedroom of a middle-class teenager and look around at all the "signs"—photos, books, music CDs, videos, computer games, posters, trophies, baseball cards, model cars, clothes, and a quilt made by a loving grandmother. The room is filled with artifacts that can be interpreted in meaningful ways. Yet the teenager who sleeps in this room can use only a small portion of these many signs when at school learning, especially in the academic classes of the curriculum. Language is the primary sign system of school, and literacy is thought, by many, to be the ability to use language to accomplish one's interactions with the world.

It is easy to understand how language came to be central to the curriculum. It is, after all, a powerful tool. Wells (1994) asserts that language is the primary sign system among all the sign systems because language enables us to check our interpretations of other sign systems with one another. We can use language to talk about the meanings presented in other sign systems. This is important, but to interact with others and to understand the world, learners need more than just proficiency with language. Learners also need facility with a full range of sign systems. And literacy needs to be equated with this full range of interpretive abilities, not just the individual's capacity for language. In the following sections, we share some of our notions of how teachers can begin to move toward an expanded notion of literacy both as individuals and in classrooms.

Learning To Be Artful

Diane Stephens (1994) used the word "artful" when she was invited to speak to a group of teachers about including more of the fine arts in their classroom instruction. She explained that her own education in the fine arts had been severely limited. Neither her parents nor her teachers thought of learning as an artful process. No one encouraged her to draw or to sing. She neither danced nor acted. So as an adult, she found these ways of knowing new and unfamiliar, even though she was making a deliberate effort to begin to appreciate and include more art and music in her life.

Diane's story resonated with us because each of us held an interest in becoming more artful, too. At first, our reasons for wanting such were academic in nature. Reading from a variety of research studies, convinced us of the value of multiple sign systems. John-Steiner (1985), for example, made a study about the thinking and learning of over one hundred highly creative and productive adults whose work involved intellectual labor—mathematicians, scientists, musicians, sculptors, choreographers, writers, and so on. She discovered through her interviews and correspondence with these creative individuals that they never worked in language alone; rather, they used many "languages of thought"—in rich combination.

Further, research such as *Language Stories and Literacy Lessons* (1984) and *I Already Know How to Read* (1996) confirmed that preschool children use multiple sign systems to support their thinking and learning. In both these studies, the children freely integrated art and writing to record their thoughts. Like most preschoolers, they made sense of the world through dramatic play, drawing, dancing, movement, singing, and other communicative systems. Even first graders in Hubbard's (1989) study of the ways children combine their use of art and writing were doing what Newkirk (1989) called "symbol-weaving." They were demonstrating the ability to work with multiple sign systems at once. These studies made us wonder why, by second and third grade, school curriculum separates the teaching and use of sign systems, so that children are no longer encouraged to draw as they write or to sing and dramatize what they know.

We were intrigued by efforts such as Harvard's Project Zero that was designed to study the impact of integrating the fine arts into high school curriculum. This study accumulated impressive data to support the claim that students learn at a higher cognitive level when art and music are incorporated into the learning experiences than when they are not. As Csikszentmihalyi (1996) explained it, not only were the students more critical and reflective about what they were learning, but also they were more engaged and motivated to concentrate and persevere at learning tasks. Other disciplined-based art educators echoed his conclusions. They explained that the payoff for integrating the fine arts and the academic curriculum was that learners became more engaged in what they were learning—asked more questions, more readily offered their own views, and more fully enjoyed learning (The Getty Center for Education in the Arts, 1993).

Our interest in research about multiple sign systems heightened our awareness of the rich variety of sign systems at work in the world around us via television, radio, movies, electronic media, and advertising. We began to wonder whether we would experience more intensity in our own learning were we to become more artful. Therefore, we each began to deliberately attend more thoughtfully to sign systems in our daily lives. Jerry and Barry started using sketch journals to capture the essence of conference presentations and teaching experiences. Kathy and Beth started using more art and music in their curricula. We also sought out artists, musicians, and dramatists for advice and help in our classrooms.

As our awareness and willingness to think and work in multiple sign systems grew more sophisticated, we realized that being artful was rejuvenating. Increasing our exposure to different sign systems changed our sensibilities to the world around us. For instance, after working with an artist during an integrated unit, Beth found herself thinking differently about taking photos. As she framed images, she began looking for the "movement" and "light" in the picture. She asked herself: What message or feeling should this picture convey? What might I do to highlight that message? These were questions she never knew to ask herself before she heard the artist ask them about paintings during the shared study. It was exciting to gain new knowledge about the elements of visual images, about how the sign system of images worked.

Each of us has now become deliberate about extending our artful knowing. We seek out conversations and teaching opportunities with specialists in the arts. We read books, watch videos, take classes, try new explorations with learners, or transmediate our thoughts into a sign system other than language. We realize there are many gaps to fill in our own ways of knowing and enjoy being learners in this new realm.

Including Sign Systems in the Curriculum

The term *sign system* originates from the discipline of semiotics, the science of interpreting signs, that is, determining their function. Sign systems—such as art, music, drama, mathematics, and language—are communication systems. We use them to construct and express meaning. They are comprised of different elements and of rules that govern how the elements are combined to make meaning. For example, painting uses the elements of color, line, and shape presented simultaneously to the viewer, while songs use tempo, pitch, and rhythms unfolding across time. We have multiple sign systems in our cultures because each sign system is effective in communicating certain kinds of messages. Music can express feelings not easily put into words; language is a better medium for humor than math; math can represent concepts not easily represented in art.

Each sign system is unique, and entire disciplines have sprung up to explain and explore their potential for making sense of the world. In our discipline-based ways of education, we include art classes, music classes, and physical education classes in the curriculum so that students have access to these multiple ways of knowing. There is, however, a basic flaw in the curricular structure in which we teach the subjects of art, of music, and of physical fitness. Certainly, these disciplines are important. They can deepen learners' understanding of how particular sign systems work and of what kind of meanings each sign system best expresses. Nevertheless, this isolated treatment of the sign systems short-circuits the kind of integrated knowing required to understand the world.

As we worked to understand what it means to implement a curriculum that views literacy in the broadest terms, we explored the notions that literacy develops simultaneously in all sign systems and that individuals make sense of their lived experience using a full range of meaning-making systems. These are very comprehensive ideas, and the best we could do was to start with what we already knew. We used strategies such as Sketch to Stretch and transmediated responses to stories (explained in Chapter 1) to begin working in multiple sign systems. From these simple strategies we could see that learners continually search for equivalencies. Asking students to find or create a piece of art to represent the meaning they attributed to a story forced them to think metaphorically, to find different ways of expressing the same idea. As they did so, they pushed beyond the literal and focused on the deeper meaning of texts. As a result, the conversations in our classrooms about the stories we read were richer, and we saw new dimensions in the students' thinking.

We began to see that the cognitive processes that were familiar to us in language were also happening in all the other sign systems—art, mathematics, music, and drama. When the learners had both the freedom to pursue their own questions and access to multiple sign systems, they flexibly "read" a wide variety of potentially meaningful texts such as paintings, science experiments, mathematical equations, songs, and sculptures and "authored" significant understandings through music, art, drama, and mathematics. As a result, they gained confidence in their ability to learn and their own unique identities. They also developed more comprehensive knowledge of media, tools, and ways of knowing.

As we added more sign systems to the curriculum, we realized the learners developed their abilities to operate in other sign systems in the same ways in which they developed as language users. When we invited them to write musical compositions, to paint murals or self-portraits, or to write mathematical problems, we had to support risk taking and invention. We also had to provide many demonstrations of the sign systems in use. Some of this, we ourselves performed as teachers. In addition, we also invited artists, musicians, storytellers, dancers, and others to work with us and to talk about the media and tools of their preferred sign systems and the nature of their creative processes.

This book details only the very first steps in what has become a lifetime inquiry for us. From this beginning, we have a clear sense that a curriculum based on inquiry and multiple ways of knowing set the stage for dramatic school change. We have gained great respect for our colleagues in the fine arts and other disciplines and recognize that they know the world in ways we do not. We believe we need to develop our abilities as teachers to collaborate with them and to support our students' literacy development in many sign systems. Otherwise, our students will grow up to be as limited in their knowing as we once were. We can say from experience that curriculum can provide students with opportunities to pursue questions across boundaries and to use multiple sign systems to gain new perspectives, process experiences, interpret texts, and imagine new possibilities and ways of being. As teachers, we can know learners more in depth, and learners can know the world more in depth when we expand our notions of literacy to include multiple sign systems and our notions of curriculum to include inquiry and multiple ways of knowing.

A colleague who read a draft of this book cautioned that we should be careful not to give the impression that we believe students should "dance through *Hamlet*." This is an interesting warning because it reflects the way the education world privileges language. Dance specialists have convinced us that there are dimensions to learning about a piece of literature such as *Hamlet* that could be best explored through dance. The question is whether we are ready to expand our definitions of literacy to be more inclusive, whether we are open to experiencing what can be known through other sign systems.

In his book, *A Democratic Classroom*, Steven Wolk (1998) tells a story about Tracy, a shy sixth grader who seemed to blend into the woodwork of his classroom. He hardly knew her, even after three months of school, and gave her C's on her first report card. Soon after that, he showed the students some examples of murals and asked them to create their own. Tracy's artwork was spectacular and demonstrated such investment and mastery over the content taught in class that he could never look at her as an "average" kid again. He goes on to say that "being human and smart is profoundly more complex and multidimensional than school makes it out to be." (p. 20) In order to understand this, and make spaces in our classrooms for the Nathaniels and Scotts and Tracys, we can begin to explore for ourselves what a person can learn from dancing *Hamlet* or painting the story of evolution. As Jerry said in the first chapter, this is an opportunity for educators to solve new problems and to learn in new ways.

Moving toward an Inquiry Framework

> The habits of schooling are deep, powerful, and hard to budge. No institution is more deeply entrenched in our habitual behavior than schools. . . . Our everyday language and metaphors are built upon all its authoritarian, filling-up-the-empty-vessel, rote-learning assumptions. . . .The kind of mental paradigm shift, the "aha" which is at the heart of learning, usually requires more than being told by an authority or shown a demonstration. . . . Those "aha" moments are hard to hold onto and often slip away in the press of daily habit. What is needed is not just new information about teaching/learning, not just more course work, but *a new way of learning about learning*. (emphasis added) (Meier, 1995, p. 140)

Meier clearly expresses reasons why the notions of inquiry and multiple ways of knowing will be difficult to advance in most school contexts. Inquiry and multiple ways of knowing are the antithesis to the kinds of programs for change currently being marketed to schools. Administrators and teachers who choose literacy instruction programs such as *Four Block* or *Success for All* seek the same learning outcomes for all students. They believe that such programs will provide teachers with the tools to meet the needs of all learners. We suspect, though, that changing the tools will never be enough to usher in education suited to the information age and the new millennium.

In schools where teachers are kept busy in their classrooms delivering programs and responding to mandates, it is almost impossible for inquiry and multiple ways of knowing to take root. As Shirley Brice Heath observes:

> Currently, teachers are isolated in their classrooms with little opportunity to talk about their solo efforts to learn; consequently their own conditions for learning mirror those they provide their students. Teachers, like their students, learn to fear cooperation with each other because of insecurities about evaluation. If teachers are to equip their students to go beyond receiving knowledge to critiquing and creating it, they must be able to model such behaviors. Accomplished modeling comes only after opportunities to play meaningful

roles in collaborative learning over a long period of time. As teachers learn from and with each other, they can gain confidence in identifying problems, as well as solving them. . . . It is the sense of being literate that enables teachers and students to stop thinking about learning and to think learning instead. (pp. 21–22)

As difficult as it may sound, we believe it is possible for individual teachers and administrators to begin the journey toward understanding and practicing inquiry and multiple ways of knowing before they have the support of the school context. In the long run, this may lead to conflict, but initially, learning about inquiry and multiple ways of knowing contributes to personal growth and change. It is a "new way of learning about learning" that is a paradigm shift away from the kind of thinking that commonly goes on in schools today. And schools can only begin to make the shift when critical numbers of individuals within them know what it means to "think learning."

In the following section, we will detail some of the ways we challenged ourselves during the study described in this book and some of what we have seen from other teachers who explore inquiry and multiple ways of knowing. One of the common threads throughout this section is the importance of finding and working with collaborators. As teachers, we are smarter when we work with others in collaborative groups; we benefit from the social aspects of learning. Even though many schools neither support nor reward collaborative teacher groups learning through engagements such as inquiry projects, sign system explorations, discussions of theoretical models, or explorations into expanded notions of literacy, we believe these learning experiences offer teachers invaluable tools for creating better classrooms, better students. We also believe we should seek the counsel of individuals whose life experiences are significantly different from our own and seek to introduce ourselves to many perspectives as we work. In short, a commitment to learn about inquiry and multiple ways of knowing amounts to a commitment to be an inquirer who is willing to learn from children and professional colleagues, to take risks, to take time, and to persevere—sometimes even in a context that provides little support.

Teacher Inquiry

Obviously, teacher research, or inquiry, is not an idea we invented, and many other educators write about it in more detail (Cochran-Smith & Lytle, 1993; Hubbard & Power, 1993; Schubert & Ayres, 1992), but we can speak from the experiences we write about in this book. Our personal inquiries went hand-in-hand with introducing inquiry and multiple ways of knowing into our curricula. As a group of colleagues, we shared the larger question of how inquiry and multiple ways of knowing could be translated into curriculum and how that would affect learning and relationships in the classrooms. Each of us found our own entry point and our own compelling questions and set about doing things to inform ourselves. Jerry observed how teachers learned from using the strategy of Sketch to Stretch and focusing on multiple sign systems in their teaching. Beth and Sue watched what happened when they set up a classroom with an inquiry and multiple sign systems framework. And Kathy and Barry profiled the learning of particular children in their classrooms as they began teaching in new ways. These personal inquiries required us to be tentative and inventive. We found ourselves conferring anxiously with one another about our assumptions. Did we really believe children learned as much when they used art as a medium for thinking as they did when they used language? How could we tell what they were learning when their products were artworks? And could we really trust children's questions? What if they never moved beyond the safety of what they already knew intimately?

Sometimes, we deliberately designed experiences for the learners that would help us answer our questions. We asked them respond to literature selections using both language and art and compared the information we received from each sign system. Other times, we stumbled onto insights by accident, for example, when the children made passing comments that drastically changed our understanding of their learning. Nathaniel did this to Barry when he first shared the tree-fort drawings he liked to do at home.

Most of the time, we were uncertain what we could say on the basis of the data we were accumulating. We had to trust the process. We saved samples of the students' work and made notes about things that they said or did. We tape-recorded interviews and talked with their parents. We hoped that when we finally found the time to sit down and sort through the children's artifacts, our records of the class learning experiences, and our reflections along the way, we would find something relevant to our questions.

For us, it was also important that we agreed to make a presentation at an NCTE conference based on our inquiries. The commitment to take our findings to an audience of knowledgeable peers forced us to do the "hard fun" of articulating our theories, describing the journeys, analyzing the data, and synthesizing what we had learned. We realized that this was one way we could start the conversations we wanted and needed to have with others outside of our little collaborative group.

When we reached the end of our first cycle of inquiry, we were pleased with ourselves for what we knew differently, not just in theory but through experience. The cycle helped us toward the habits of being more open to one another's ideas and the voices of the learners, and more deliberate about documenting our journeys and experiences with learners. We found that we liked thinking about teaching and learning from an inquiry stance because it gave us a reason to collaborate as professionals, and it made teaching intellectually stimulating in ways that were new and exciting to us.

Our own inquiries provided a place for us to learn about our own learning and to gain insights that we could transfer back to our work with the children. Barry, for example, started his inquiry by learning alongside a chef, an artist, and a dancer and consequently discovered how thinking looked in other sign systems. Beth and Sue became very aware of the kinds of choices inquirers make—choices such as what to observe, what to write down, what to reflect on in writing, and what to gather and look at over time. Sometimes, we realized that we had to have an experience more than once in order to trust its meaning, and more than anything, we recognized that we needed to write or draw or make records of our thinking often, as Kathy did by assessing Scott.

We learned that teacher inquiry is one way teachers can facilitate their move toward implementing a curriculum based on inquiry. As we pursued our own questions, we experienced the tensions and cognitive demands of the inquiry process. We experienced how the inquiry process cycles and recycles—sometimes with false starts and dead ends—and how it requires the thoughtful responses and collaborative thinking of colleagues. We realized that inquiry is self-directed and time-consuming intellectual work, exactly the kind of work we want our students to be doing. And we basically internalized the logic and rhythm of the inquiry process through experience. This kind of understanding makes teaching from an inquiry perspective much more possible.

Learning about Inquiry through Classroom Practice

Our roots as teachers of inquiry were laid down in the context of learning about reading and writing. In 1988, Harste, Short, and Burke introduced us to the "authoring cycle" in their book *Creating Classrooms for Authors*. They explained how reading and writing could be thought of and taught as purposeful social processes propelled by a variety of subprocesses, such as having life experiences, drafting personal writing, creating personal interpretations, sharing, critiquing, and revising. According to their framework, one complete cycle of the reading or authoring process could take days, even weeks, to complete.

When we began to incorporate the reading and authoring cycles into our teaching, fascinating new insights emerged. For example, we could tell that our students were learning more when the day was not broken into small time blocks for separate subject instruction. They benefited more from having time to interact with each other and with their reading and writing than they did from teacher-directed lessons and practice worksheets. We saw how the level of engagement changed for the learners and for us as teachers. Instead of plodding through a day of lessons that were superfluous to the learners, we worked on discovering how to stay at the edges of what the children knew and on creating the context and experiences to push beyond those edges.

In retrospect, we can see that moving to the reading and authoring cycles set up a context wherein we as teachers became active learners. We had to learn to "kidwatch" (Y. Goodman, 1978), and we had to hone our knowledge of the developmental aspects of learning to read and write. We also began to see the power of giving children choices and helping them to follow their own pathways of development. Each day brought new challenges, and we began to get more deliberate about resolving our tensions. We began choosing one aspect of the process to study and work on at a time. And we were validated in our efforts by the professional journals as they began to fill up with rich stories of inquiry about children's reading and writing.

The more we learned about teaching reading and writing via a social process, the more it made sense to think about teaching other parts of the curriculum in the same way. When Short, Harste, and Burke (1996) revised their book to include the inquiry process, we were ready to make the leap to inquiry cycles. We began planning and teaching focused studies, consciously walking our students through related engagements, asking them to practice observing, making connections, investigating, exploring tensions, presenting, reflecting, and taking social action.

Focused studies are units of study organized around the collaborative inquiry process. They are deliberate journeys that take the learners through many smaller cycles of meaning construction in search of connections and coherence. The goals of a focused study are to ask an essential question, to delve into as many perspectives related to the question as possible, and to construct a coherent network of information that sets the stage for learners to ask their own questions and launch their own inquiries.

It can be helpful to think of a focused study as the process whereby a group of learners constructs the whole of knowing about something so they can return individually and study the parts that most interest them. Focused studies enlist the members of the learning community into service for the good of the group. When each group member contributes his or her perspectives, talents, knowledge, and constructive work, the pool of shared knowledge and experiences grows exponentially. So do the opportunities to make connections and be reflective. Everyone is focused on finding ways to answer the question that has no easy answers. The work challenges the learners to be cohesive and yet to think for themselves.

The teacher's task during a focused study is to guide the shared inquiry as it evolves so that the learners end up developing deep conceptual understandings. This requires a real sense of timing and a feel for the underlying processes of collaborative inquiry. Students need a certain amount of time to "wander and wonder." They need opportunities to think and create things for themselves. They need opportunities to rub their thinking up against the thinking of others. And they need time to synthesize ideas and information, to cast them into different sign systems and to explain them to their peers and others. Both the students and the teacher need to see concrete evidence of the thinking and learning going on so that they can be reflective about what is being learned and what still needs to be explored or challenged.

In our own teaching, we learned how to orchestrate focused studies by first orchestrating smaller cycles of inquiry, such as literature discussions, response projects, mathematical problem solving, and science explorations. These discipline-based inquiries provided the students with practice in assuming an inquiry stance and collaborating during process work. To move up to the level of focused studies, we started to plan so that all of these smaller cycles of inquiry had a coherence to them that supported the students in developing bigger conceptual wholes. And we started to structure learning time in uninterrupted blocks and to work through cycles of individual thinking and creating, small-group thinking and creating, and whole-group experiences and reflective time.

Our experiences with inquiry-based curriculum have led us to think of focused studies as a sort of "zone of proximal development" (Vygotsky, 1978) for our students and ourselves. These thematic units of study provide learners with experiences in doing many different kinds of thinking and considering many different perspectives. Focused studies provide demonstrations of critical thinking and revision and give a new sense of the depth of understanding learners can construct when the underlying processes of inquiry are layered upon one another. The richness of the social learning process transforms the internal structures of the learners. Just as learners borrow language from those around them to think about the world, learners borrow the processes and perspectives introduced in focused studies and use them to accomplish their own personal learning.

When we taught from textbooks, we focused on teaching content. As teachers, we thought our responsibility was to help students learn the concepts and information considered significant by the experts in the disciplines. When we taught multidisciplinary thematic units, we took on the added responsibility of fostering connections among concepts and information. Teaching focused studies, these units of curriculum that we co-constructed with the learners, has taught us that we can do far more than teach concepts and connections. We can teach learners and ourselves how to learn. When curriculum becomes a process of social knowledge construction, learners are not simply absorbing and applying knowledge. Rather, they take ownership of the process of generating knowledge and creating theories about how the knowledge fits together into larger wholes.

Communities of learners generate such rich varieties of information and perspectives that the learners are much more likely to apply a kind of logic semioticians call abduction (Cunningham, 1992). Abduction begins when the learners encounter something their current theories and knowledge cannot explain. They have to tolerate ambiguity while they collect more information and revise or totally reconfigure their schema. None of this is necessarily conscious on the part of the learners, but learners do recognize those "aha" moments when something suddenly makes sense in a new way. And they do come to understand learning as an ongoing, generative process of making connections, looking for larger patterns, and having tentative theories that are open to revision.

The role of the teacher in an inquiry-based curriculum is to possess not only expert knowledge about different disciplines but also expert knowledge about how learners learn. As teachers, we demonstrate what a person with advanced knowledge can do to support other learners. We share what we know about learning as we work alongside students by thinking out loud about our choices of strategies and engagements and posing our own questions. We demonstrate how students can pursue their own questions by pursuing our own, constantly gathering data and sharing our analyses. We inquire into the learning of the students as we track their thinking and questions and keep track of the tools and resources they are using. We also expose students to perspectives that are missing from their view and to expert knowledge that relates to their questions. In all this work, we talk with the students so that we know the sense they make of learning. And before long, the students do all the things that we do as teachers for each other. As a result, the learning community becomes a powerful place to learn.

In many ways, teaching that revolves around inquiry is artful in ways teaching out of textbooks could never be. It requires the orchestration of many dimensions of learning all at once, much like working in a sign system. In our explorations and attempts to operate from an inquiry perspective, we found that we knew when the teaching was working in much the same way as we know when a piece of music, or literature, or art is aesthetic. We felt it. We knew intuitively, and so did the students. It was hard at first to get to these moments of teaching and learning. We had limited repertoires of strategies for supporting the underlying processes such as negotiating meanings, critiquing drafts, revising, and presenting. We had few strategies for teaching about the media and tools of various sign systems, and only simple notions of how we could document the learning of the children. As we explored inquiry-based teaching, our repertoires of strategies improved, and we learned more about learning by inquiring into each student's learning.

We cannot know for certain what goes on inside children. We can only listen to their questions and explanations, learn about their lives outside of school, observe their ways of interacting with other people and the world, and predict how we can best support them based on our own theories of the world. This continual process is full of frustrations, disappointments, surprises, and wonders. This kind of teaching never stops being demanding cognitive and emotional work, but when we begin to understand it as an ongoing process, we can relax into it. And relish our good fortune to have life's work that is purposeful and artful.

Planning for Focused Studies

Planning a focused study begins with thinking about networks of knowledge. This is not an easy or common practice in education. We tend not to focus on the "wholes" of our knowing, but rather on parts, such as the science concepts, the mathematics skills, or the language proficiencies. We have to begin to recognize that we have "whole" constructed understandings that serve as our schema for predicting the world, such as our understandings of violence and hate, democracy, or life. Some curriculum experts tell us that there are only a handful of concepts that encompass all knowledge, such as the concepts of change, force, and interdependence. When we plan a focused study, we aim at these large overarching knowledge knots that connect so many different layers of information and ways of knowing. This is what makes focused studies so powerful. They result in knowing at a more complex level than curriculum that focuses on the parts of knowing, not the wholes.

Because we are in somewhat unfamiliar territory when we try to identify the focus for a focused study, it is hard to describe exactly how we decide on a topic or essential question. Sometimes we start with a concept, theme, or topic and back our way into an essential question and a sense of the larger whole we hope the students can construct. On a couple occasions, we have started with a song that we found particularly meaningful and built the focused study from all the connections suggested by the song. In other instances, we have asked ourselves what questions we wished our students could answer when they graduated from our schools or what questions would move the focus of our curriculum out into the community around the school and set up the potential for social action. In every effort to plan a focused study, we have had to be willing to choose a thread of some sort in order to get started and to trust that the process of planning would help us to clarify the larger unit of meaning we were striving to reconstruct.

Once we have a notion of what we want our focused study to help the students understand, we go to work clarifying the connections and possibilities of the topic and essential questions for ourselves. This takes at least a couple of weeks, because it takes time for the ideas to percolate in our heads, time for talking to colleagues and researching the topic, and time for drawing maps of the territory for ourselves. We make lists and webs and models and organizers—anything that helps us to grasp the whole of the focused study territory. Mostly we do this kind of planning in sketch journals or daybooks that we keep within reach since we find ourselves having insights without notice and ideas that run through our minds when we least expect them. Some of this capturing-of-the-whole also involves deliberately sorting through the proficiency guides and standard documents that frame our teaching and identifying the most relevant and likely skills and knowledge we can teach in the context of the focused study. Our students do well on standardized tests when we teach via focused studies because the students' learning is deep and comprehensive. And we do keep specific testable skills in mind and make sure the students are sufficiently prepared for the all-important tests.

At the same time as we are taking note of connections and trying to formulate an essential question or questions to guide the focused study, we are also collecting resources and teaching strategies that are likely to be useful during the study. We gather armloads of children's books, often up to a hundred or more, that address some aspect of the study. We also collect other media such as music CDs and videos or Web sites, information about guest speakers or artists, and raw materials for projects and multiple sign systems experiences, science equipment, mathematics manipulatives, and so on. Often the work of collecting these resources sparks new ideas and connections.

We also begin talking to the students about the topic of the focused study and get information about their related experiences and conceptions or misconceptions. In large part, our starting points depend on the learners. We begin to ask ourselves what we need to do to get the learners to begin thinking about the focus of the study and understanding the dimensions of the question.

Once we have a sense of what the unit can accomplish, we begin to plan for the conversations and processes we predict will support the students in constructing knowledge and finding coherence. We start a "planning-to-plan" process wherein we list actual experiences and engagements that we think we can use to help the students develop their knowledge. As we do this, we imagine the journey we are going to take with the students. At first, we like to do things that awaken their sensibilities and call their attention to the edges of their thinking. During the first week or two of a focused study we like to immerse students in engagements designed to raise issues and questions, to stir up doubt and wonder, and to present new possibilities. For example, we may plan to study a book or a song or have a community-based experience that introduces new information and ideas. We may set up invitations that introduce new sign system opportunities for thinking metaphorically, such as a water-painting center or a keyboard exploration. Actually, the possibilities for initiating experiences are endless—videos, Internet sites, guest speakers, reenactments, field trips—anything that will signal to students that the inquiry is getting underway and that there is significant learning work to be done.

When we plan, we also ask ourselves how the inquiry will be documented. What will the learners do to be reflective and to create an "audit trail," a tangible record of their learning journey? (Harste & Vasquez, 1998) We decide on some strategy or strategies for making a record of the process. We may have the students keeping journals or learning logs. They may have large individual chart papers that they gradually fill with everything from drawings to written reflections to photographs of their projects. They may be continually adding items to their web pages or videotaping their reflections, or any combination of these strategies for being thoughtful about their own learning process and insights.

As the focused study gets underway, we work to understand what sense the students make of the conceptual whole we are trying to develop, and respond to their interests and knowledge by offering engagements that connect to and extend them. For example, Sue and Beth started a focused study designed to teach two big chunks of curriculum—fairy tales and the natural environment (see Appendix B: Real and Make-Believe). As they started the unit, they were not quite sure what the essential question should be, but they discovered quickly that the first graders were somewhat fuzzy on the difference between fact and fiction. The children were puzzled by John Scieszka's book, *The True Story of the Three Little Pigs* (1991). Leslie asked her peers which story was "really true"— the original story of the three little pigs or the story as told by Scieszka that makes the wolf look like the good guy. And the children were genuinely confused when Sue dressed up like Cinderella and greeted them one morning in the classroom. She had her hair in a kerchief and an apron tied around her waist with a single high heel in the pocket. The children listened intently to her story about meeting the prince and gave her suggestions for how she might find her missing shoe. Sue stepped out of the room to take off the kerchief and apron, and when she returned, a handful of children circled her to look over her clothes. "We think that was really you, Mrs. Hamilton." But there was doubt in their voices. They were not sure yet where to draw the line between real and imaginary.

When we provide thought-provoking initiating experiences and offer children a full range of sign systems for thinking about and expressing their ideas and responses to these experiences, we open a window to the thinking of the learners. The first graders revealed that they were interested in the concept of "real versus not real"; they were trying to make sense of the difference between fact and fiction. Knowing this, Beth and Sue started to offer a rich variety of experiences and to host conversations aimed at helping the children to figure out, to talk about, and to demonstrate that they understood the difference between fact and fiction. They planted seeds and acted out the story of the gingerbread boy and talked about the difference between real and make-believe. They read countless fairy tales and made charts about the characters, settings, and so on. Next, they wrote stories that incorporated the elements they could identify in fairy tales and conducted inquiry projects about the real world, pursuing questions such as "How was the earth formed?" "What makes day and night?" "How does it rain?" "How do birds fly?" "What happens to a seed after the plant grows out of it?" At the end of the focused study, the children were clear about the difference between real and make-believe, and they had authored both factual and fictional pieces of writing.

It is very difficult to draw a model of a focused study process because no two focused study cycles are the same. Once we interpret the students' responses to our initial engagements, we begin to think about how to build the conceptual wholes we have in mind from the basis of their knowledge and developmental abilities. We know that the work of developing deeper understandings depends on having many coherent experiences and intellectual engagement in processes that help learners see many perspectives and make connections. We involve the learners in strategies such as literature study, authoring cycles, sign system explorations, discipline-based inquiry, authentic problem solving, and social action because we continue to gain insight into their thinking. We can, therefore, continually add to and adjust our offerings. Also because they have the support of their peers as thinkers, and they experience the power of revision and reflection.

When we plan a focused study, we give particular thought to a culminating experience. We want to bring closure to the unit with an experience that will help the students pull all the pieces of the study together and put them in the role of teacher as they create presentations or exhibitions that communicate what they have learned. We think about who the audience will be for their public demonstrations of learning and often use this time to bring in parents and people from the community or other students in the school. As much as possible, we try to create authentic opportunities to inform a public so that students can see that their learning has significance beyond the classroom. Students find it compelling to know there is an event like a family night or an exhibition fair with an audience waiting to hear what they have learned.

Culminating experiences bring closure to a process that could go on indefinitely, but we do not think of them as the end so much as the beginning. If we have done our work well, the students will see ways to extend their new knowledge into social action. They will have new commitments to act on, and we can invent novel ways to use their understandings for the good of their families, school, and communities.

Final Thoughts

In the first chapter of this book, Jerry outlines points of departure— places to begin a new way of thinking about teaching and learning. The classroom stories that follow tell the stories of Beth and Sue, Kathy and Barry— four teachers' initial attempts to put theory into practice. The stories are interesting in their own right, but they are also the tip of an iceberg. They comprise visible signs of something deeper and more complex.

Theory based on inquiry and multiple ways of knowing changes the basic notions of curriculum and knowing, as well as the quality of human relationships formed in learning communities. At this point, we are still working to understand these changes, and much of what we have learned is not really evident in our stories. The experiences we describe in the book form our starting points, and the inquiry process has taken us to understandings beyond our initial experiences.

For example, we now understand that curriculum is the work of a learning community, not just the work of individuals. We are social learners, and we need one another to make the most of our potential to learn. We have learned this as teachers. We are better learners when we collaborate with our colleagues. We also see how the social network of the class can be used to support children's in-depth engagement with learning. As teachers, we can choose processes and strategies that fit the occasion. Transmediation, for example, tends to enhance voice. Students who are silent or unre-markable when asked to respond in language, often shine in another sign system. Choice or a shared interest spurs any process. Two readers sharing a text can integrate reading, conversations, and reflection. And difference can act as a stimulus for learning. These are the tools of a teacher who is creating a democratic classroom where learners are invited to take ownership and responsibility for their own learning and the learning of the entire community.

Communication is the key to the health and power of a learn-ing community. Learners can understand the purposes of what they are asked to do, and teachers can know the learners well enough to build bridges between their ways of knowing and the school's. Like Kathy and Barry, teachers will be perplexed by students' responses to learning engagements and social situations. This theory of teach-ing suggests that teachers should be more tentative in their "read-ing" of students, more exploratory and open to multiple interpreta-tions. When Scott balked at writing a letter to his classmate and complained that it was a nonsensical thing to do since he would see the classmate the following day at school, we might possibly inter-pret his response in several different ways. Initially, we might think that he is lazy and good at making excuses. With some reflection, we might conclude that writing is a burden for Scott and that he prefers oral language experiences. We might eventually come to think of Scott as very pragmatic and driven by an ethic of efficiency.

When we think in terms of multiple interpretations, we realize that we have to gather more information about the learner. We may want to talk with Scott about his resistance to writing and find out what he can tell us. Or perhaps we would change the book he was asked to read to one about jets and see what happens. Or maybe we would look back through anecdotal notes to see if there is a pattern in Scott's responses that indicate that he favors oral language over written. In other words, as teachers we constantly work to under-stand the relationship of the learner to the learning of the commu-nity and seek to support the learner in having an equal voice and making a significant contribution to the learning of the entire group.

Another challenge of a theory based on inquiry and multiple ways of knowing is the challenge of keeping knowledge whole. We have very little experience with thinking of knowledge as insepa-rable from the knower or the systems of knowing. Each individual creates personal internal structures that borrow their forms from the sign systems and knowledge of other people. The sign systems, knowledge systems, and cultural systems at work in the world around us support certain relationships of power and privilege. There is no place to stand outside these meaning-making systems that carry with them messages about gender, class, race, and power.

When we borrow signs, or information, from these systems to construct our own meanings, we also borrow invisible assumptions about power and privilege that are inescapably laced into these systems. As we borrow, we are indoctrinated. What is outside us is also inside us.

Meanwhile, each learner is also situated in a social context that affects his or her access to certain kinds of knowledge and purposes for learning. In the face of this complexity, we believe we have to rethink what we do to support learners as knowledge constructors. We are trying to learn how we can treat learning as part of living, rather than just as a school activity, and how we can appreciate the diversity of learners who meet in our classrooms.

In the long run, all of this is about democracy. It concerns how the larger community is going to operate to learn and evolve together—a far cry from the individual competitive framework currently in schools. As Jerry puts it, these new ideas and practices disrupt the text of schooling. They force us to start having hard conversations.

As we move on from this point, we are developing a deep commitment to critical literacy and social action. We believe teachers can help learners recognize that the social practices they borrow from the culture outside of school are often harmful to some people. Luke (1995) suggests we can do this by attending to the face-to-face aspects of literacy. We have to help learners become aware of the choices they make—when to speak, when to be silent, what to say—and how their intentions affect the learning community. Gallas (1994) for example, writes about the "bad boys" in her class. These are boys who vie with the teacher for power in the classroom—silencing some children, harassing others, and distracting many. As she researches these boys in action, she concludes, "the classroom is only a mirror reflecting the problems of discrimination, misunderstanding, and violence" of the larger society. In response, she continues:

> By paying close attention to the stories they tell, draw, dance, write, and enact, I am more able to include their divergent worldview in the culture of the classroom. My hope, as they see that school is not a battleground, is that they will begin to alter their picture of where their own personal power lies. In the end, I want these boys to experience how powerful it is to belong and fully commit oneself to the creation of a dynamic learning community, where rather than struggling continuously to assert their superiority and control, they work to fuel the intensity and excitement of everyone's participation. (p. 70)

In part, the ability to re-culture a learning community depends on our personal knowledge of the systems of domination and discrimination. We have to understand culture, history, our multicultural world, and the social and political forces that act on our lives. We cannot help learners break through the barriers of race, gender, and social class if we do not understand the socially and ideologically constructed nature of sign systems, knowledge, and society and do not consciously ask how our own daily decisions and practices contribute to the maintenance of these systems. We must understand the cultural values and practices of our learners (Ladson-Billings, 1996) and think about how their cultural frameworks can be both embraced and challenged.

Given the whole language community's history of generating new perspectives and affecting change, we think the work of incorporating inquiry and multiple ways of knowing is a step toward social justice that we can make by working thoughtfully in classrooms and sharing what we learn. We need to tell each other our stories about having conversations that matter with the learners and about interrogating the values that stand in the way of our appreciating the strengths and perspectives of each learner. Stories such as Dyson's (1995) story about Tina, an African American third grader, who recognizes that the boys in her class do not write stories with female heroines. It is hard for Tina to create a personal identity that is caring and powerful when her peers operate on the "X-men" values borrowed from the commercial culture. These are the subtle and slippery ways the culture reproduces itself. It slips into the learning community as part and parcel of the learners' identities, and we can only see it when we heighten our own awareness of how the larger culture shapes the learners and relationships in our communities.

The whole language community has supported us as we have learned to value the social construction of knowledge, to be open to changing ourselves and our practices, and to never take things for granted. The whole language community is a community of learners who continue to push themselves to make a difference, even though it is sometimes hard to discern how things are changing from our local situations.

We love the kind of wide-awakeness and imagination that have enriched our lives as we have explored inquiry and multiple ways of knowing. We love the ways we know learners and ourselves better. And we are hopeful that these ways of knowing are the beginnings of more equitable and caring school cultures and communities. We invite everyone who reads this book to join the community of teachers committed to making schools and society the kind of places where we want to live and learn. We have so much to learn from each other.

Appendix A
COLONIAL AMERICA:
A Focused Study

Focusing Question:

What was it like to live in this country when it was new?

Initiating Experiences:

Activities that help partici-pants reflect on their personal experiences and knowledge in formulating predictions concerning the unit of study.

* Museum
We gathered a collection of artifacts that weren't necessarily authentic, but representative of Colonial American times. Such things as: a wooden spoon, shells, rabbit fur, beads, seeds, Indian corn, gourd, bow, basket, wool, a spinning spindle, etc. All these items were mounted on a large peg board. The children chose an item they be-lieved they could tell the group about and we began by making labels and guesses about the use of each item.

* Portrait Painter
Beth researched portrait painters of the era and came to class dressed and playing the role of a portrait painter from the late 1700s. She talked to the children about her life and asked one to sit for a portrait. She described the kinds of things she attended to as an artist and demonstrated drawing a portrait.

* Generation After Generation
Each child brought in a family tree. We used it to graph the number of years between generations in all the families. From the graph, we could see that an average generation was 30 years. We used intervals of 30 and counted back to find out there have been 16 generations since Columbus came in 1492. We used potato stamps of people to make a visual representation of this.

* Three Ways to Tell A Story
We shared the Columbus story in three sign systems. Once as a picture book. Once as a poem. And once as a number story using a drawing and numbers like miles, the number of days, dates, and numbers of men and ships.

* A Visit from "The Pilgrim Lady"
Sue's friend, Wendy, came dressed as a colonial woman and told the children about her life. She read them a book about corn, *Corn is Maize* and helped them to make corn bread.

Devices for Organiz-ing and Sharing:

Artifacts that support the manipulation and preservation of accumulating information. These should highlight relation-ships being explored and should reflect the tools/methods of the knowledge domains being studied.

* Time Line
Using our generations as a unit, we constructed a time line to start sequencing events in a visual way.

* Learning Logs
At the end of each day, the children wrote their thoughts or about their experiences in their learning logs.

*Portfolios
Many of the artifacts produced during the unit are being stored in notebooks where the students comment on them and can look across engagements that have been meaningful to them.

Reflective Learning Experiences:

Invitations:
Opportunities to make meaning using a variety of sign systems and texts.

* Clothes Make the Person
Costumes from the period are put in the corner with an invitation to read the book *Sarah Morton's Day*. The children dress in the clothes and pretend that they are colonists. They are invited to write the stories that emerge.

* Quilts
A text set about quilts, a set of pattern blocks, a tape recording called Grandmother's Patchwork Quilt, pattern sheets, and fabric are some of the items that are available at this invitation. The children are invited to browse, listen, and make their own creations.

* Curious Curators
The museum is easily rearranged and the children are invited to sort the items and talk about their categories. They can also draw and write about the items and slip their information into our museum handbook which will be a guide to visitors.

* Reflection Center
Here the children are invited to use scrap materials to rethink the experiences they have been involved with. They generally recreate artifacts or create new artifacts to go with familiar texts.

* Portrait Gallery
A cloth-covered board with postcard portraits from the era and a text set of books are situated by the easel where the children are invited to draw themselves or a friend. There are pastels or crayons to draw with.

* Flannel Board Math
Men and a ship are available at the flannel board for making up problems. How many on the ship? How many more come aboard? How many in all? The board is divided into quadrants and children are also invited to group them and count.

* Walk-in Wigwam
We used tent poles to create the basic structure of a wigwam. The children were invited to help weave mats to cover the outside. The children were then invited to use the wigwam as a place to think about what they knew of Indian life as they pretended to be Indians living there.

* Making Music
Children were invited to make simple instruments like drums and rattles, or to use small flutes. They used these to accompany themselves as they read, especially poems.

Shared Reading:
Social group shares and supports individual members in considering what might be significant aspects and relationships within the text.

* Literature Circles
The children work with a small group to read and make meaning from a text they have chosen. Our titles included: *Barn Dance, Drummer Hoff, Quilt Story, Oxcart Man,* and *Pumpkin, Pumpkin.*

* Poetry
We read the poem *Christopher Columbus* as a whole group and discussed rhythm and rhyme. Then individuals chose poems from the collection called *Dancing Teepees* to copy and learn for their own enjoyment.

Conceptually Related Texts:

Multiple and varied sources of information that provide alternative perspectives and create opportunities for complex connections.

* Text Sets
Our library for the unit included text sets built around the following topics: quilts, Indians, changes, time, portraits, Colonial America, making music, farms, and starting a new country.

* Indian Dances
We learned to do the Corn Dance and the Deer Dance, both dances which the Indians did as part of their rituals and celebrations.

* Indian Legends
We discovered a rich source of information in the form of Indian legends and read many of these aloud to the children.

Systematic Doing:

Applying questions, tools, and methods of a field of study to a specific issue.

* Exploring Text Sets
Small groups chose a text set and made a graffiti board of the things they knew related to that topic. Then they browsed the books and added to their information, thereby demonstrating some of the possible things others might learn by using the text sets.

* Learner Presentations
Small groups generated five important insights they had gained up to that time in the unit. Each group chose one of these ideas to transpose into a presentation for the class. Skits, poetry, constructing teepees, and individual pictures were some of the modes of presentation.

* Corn Husking
Pairs of children stripped an ear of corn, counting the leaves, describing the silk, and then cutting the corn off the cob for making succotash. The class helped generate a large chart with new vocabulary and labels for the parts of a corn plant and a graph of the number of leaves on each ear.

* Portrait Read-Around
The children were asked to talk about the differences and similarities they saw in a set of their portrait drawings. They noticed what others attended to and talked about the things they liked about individual portraits. Generated what they considered to be the guidelines for portrait drawing.

* Inquiry Projects
The children were encouraged to think about their own interests and to choose a focus for inquiry. They then worked in small groups to discover all they could related to their inquiry and presented their learning as a group to the class.

* Field Trips
The class visited the Children's Museum exhibit on settling America and spent a day at the Conners Prairie Settlement where actors relive the past with the children. In each experience, the children had to act as social scientists, piecing together an understanding from what they could see and hear.

Culminating Experience

Activities that help the participants reflect on their current experience and opinions in constructing their understanding of the unit of study.

* Thanksgiving Feast
The parents were invited to bring a dish to share and the children prepared a short performance. The parents got to share a video tape of the childrens' inquiry projects and the students showed them their work.

Appendix B
REAL AND MAKE-BELIEVE:
A FOCUSED STUDY
How does the world of fairy tales compare to the real world in which we live?

Generative Experiences:

Activities that help the participants focus on the semantic territory of the study by supporting connections with past experiences and the knowledge of other learners. Also demonstrating potentials for knowing more.

MAKE BELIEVE

A Visit From Cinderella: Using a head scarf, a broom, and long apron, Sue transformed herself into Cinderella and greeted the children with a slipper tucked in her pocket. She asked if they knew where her other shoe might be and spent 15 minutes as the character of Cinderella, answering their questions and hearing their connections to the story.

Letters From Fairytale Land: Each child received a letter from a fairytale character written to highlight the character's point of view, i.e. Baby Bear complained about the mean child, Goldilocks. The letters asked for advice or information.

Characters Come to Life: Teachers were recruited to dress and act like fairy tale characters and to drop off their stories for the children. Visitors included Little Red Riding Hood, Goldilocks, and the Giant. An invitation was extended to parents and two parents came in and read to the class as a character.

The Jolly Postman: This book links a number of fairy tales into one story and set the stage for thinking of the characters beyond the

REAL

Planting Seeds: The children planted a variety of seeds—marigolds in front of the school, green peppers in plastic cups, and bean seeds in baggies. These activities spawned discussions on weather, irrigation, photosynthesis, garden mapping, counting and graphing.

The Valdez Oil Spill: After sharing a book about the Alaskan Oil Spill of 1989, the children experienced the separation of oil and water. They were then asked to invent ways to separate the oil and water.

The 3 R's of Ecology: Recycle, reuse, and reduce—These concepts were introduced by a parent who set up a miniature recycling center in the class. She explained the different markings and materials which were recyclable and encouraged the children to bring these items to school to be sorted and recycled.

Arbor Day: The class participated in a school-wide Arbor Day celebration. Children reused paper corn stalks from their Colonial America Focused Study to create costumes and presented a poem about the exchange of oxygen and carbon dioxide.

confines of their stories. The children acted this book out by having small groups play each of the households visited by the postman.

A Fresh Perspective: The children read stories with a unique view, i.e. *The True Story of the Big Bad Wolf.* Sue also read them *Snail's Spell.* Following a discussion of point of view, pairs of students were asked to assume the roles of reporter and witness to one of the fairy tales. Their scenarios were video-taped for further discussion.

Devices for Organizing and Sharing:
Activities that support participants in thinking and presenting what they have learned to others.

Learning Scrolls: The children used these each day to write about their learning.

Good/Bad Murals: The children recognized the good/bad contrast among story tale characters. They used a variety of art materials to create characters and placed them on the palace mural: "good" characters on one side and "bad" on the other. They wrote a word balloon for each figure to explain the placement.
     A good/bad mural was also created in the ecology study.

Portfolios: Stories, drawings, and other artifacts produced during this unit were stored in cereal boxes. The children were asked to sort through their artifacts and to choose a few that illustrated what was important to them about their learning. These were collected in a notebook and shared with others.

Reflective Learning Experiences:

Invitations:
Opportunities to make meaning using a variety of sign systems and texts.

Established Centers: A few centers continue: *a writing center* with paper and pens—used as a place to write letters; *the computer*—with software for math or word processing; *the classroom library*—stocked with fairy tales and text sets, *a math center*—manipulatives and invitations; *a keyboard*—for composing; and *the reflection center*—the child is free to create what s/he chooses.

When You Wish Upon A Star: This was a homework invitation. Each child took home a cutout of a star with a tail and printed the name of a fairy tale they read with their family on the points of a star. Then he or she added a wish on the tail and brought it back for display.

The Neighborhood: Using a large paper base and playdough, the children created a model of fairytale

The Palace: Large paper covered an entire wall in the classroom. Students were invited to draw the palace from *Cinderella*. Dress-up clothing such as a ball dress and suit coat invited the children to act out and embellish the stories.

The Post Office: The letter writing activity of the class necessitated the creation of a post office where stamps could be purchased with play money, objects weighed to determine postage, addresses checked, and letters routed and delivered.

land as they envisioned it after reading the *Jolly Postman*.

Edible, Incredible Seeds: This invitation featured an assortment of seeds from the kitchen—caraway seeds, celery seeds, beans, rice, poppy seeds, etc. The children were invited to smell and taste and also use the seeds to make mosaics—an art technique they were inventing for themselves with scraps of paper.

Shared Reading:
Social group shares and supports individual members in considering what might be significant aspects and relationships within the text.

Literature Circles: Small groups worked with the teacher, reading and discussing texts. We started with fairy tales and went to real stories of ecology/environment. Titles included: *Cinderella, Little Red Riding Hood, Jack and the Beanstalk, A Tree Is Nice, The Giving Tree, A Snail's Spell.*

Literature Circles with Different Versions of a Story: A few of the children thoroughly enjoyed comparing versions of fairy tales. These children chose to be in groups where everyone got a different version of the same story and they spent their time comparing language, illustrations, characters, etc.

Conceptually Related Texts:
Multiple and varied sources of information that provide alternative perspectives and create opportunities for complex connections.

Turtle on Long Pond: The set of materials included a beautiful nonfiction book about the daily life of a turtle, a couple of other turtle books, a turtle puppet made out of a sock and a butter dish, and a variety of art materials, i.e. pipe cleaners, felt, fur, paper, sticks, and so on. The children studied the books and used the materials to re-enact the turtle's day.

Students' Choice: The children had become interested in how our choice of read-aloud books augmented the other things we were learning in the focused studies. They began to sign-up and take turns bringing in a book they could read to the class that would add to the knowledge base.

Systematic Doing:
Applying questions, tools, and methods of a field of study to a specific issue.

Inquiry Projects: The children were encouraged to develop their own questions about our world and to choose a focus for inquiry. They then worked in small groups to discover all they could related to

Science Observations: There were a variety of seeds planted and each child was responsible for charting the growth of a plant. They measured, used graph paper, drew pictures and wrote about their plants.

their inquiry and presented their learning as a group to the class.

Math Journaling: Each day a math problem was on the board and the children used their journals to write about their thinking as they solved the problem. These journals were then shared in small groups.

Bookmaking: The children wrote fractured fairy tales or anything of their choice. After these had gone through the authoring cycle, the children typed them on the computer and made their stories into illustrated books.

Maps: The concept of mapping was introduced with the *Jolly Postman* and the children did story maps of their literature books.

Organizational Flow Charts: After studying the postal system, the children made charts to show how mail moved from one place to another.

Making Music: Here the children could use an electronic keyboard to write their own music. There were head-phones for their independent use, and often students shared what they wrote during a sharing time later in the day.

Culminating Experience:
An activity which helps the participants reflect on their current experience and opinions in constructing their understanding of the unit of study.

Portfolio Night: The children were invited to bring their parents in to help them sort through all the artifacts they had saved during the focused study. When the parents came, they were instructed to help the child choose three significant things to put into the final portfolio and to write a reflection with the child about each choice.

Inquiry Fair: Each small group set up their demonstrations and exhibitions from their inquiries all around the room. Two classes of fifth graders visited and went to each group, listening to their presentations and asking questions.

Bibliography

Authors' Note: While writing this book, we often talked about our indebtedness to the whole language thought collective, whose work provided us with foundational knowledge. We decided that one way to acknowledge this thought collective would be to cite their publications in a specific section of the bibliography. We hope this will be helpful to inquirers who are looking for other like-minded resources.

The Whole Language/ Inquiry/Multiple Ways of Knowing Thought Collective

Berghoff, B. (1993). Moving toward aesthetic literacy in the first grade. In D. Leu & C. Kinzer (Eds.), *Examining central issues in literacy research, theory, and practice* (pp. 217–226). Chicago, IL: National Reading Conference.

Burke, C. (1991). "Great concepts in language: Curriculum and cognition." Bloomington, IN: Doctoral seminar, Indiana University.

Burke, C. & Short, K. (1995). *Creating inquiry curriculum.* Conference presentation at the Whole Language Umbrella Conference, San Diego, CA.

Goodman, K. (1967). Reading: A psycholinguistic guessing game. *Journal of the Reading Specialist, 4* (1), 126–135.

Goodman, K. (1996). *On reading: A common-sense look at the nature of language and the science of reading.* Portsmouth, NH: Heinemann.

Goodman, Y. (1978). Kidwatching: An alternative to testing. *National Elementary School Principal, 57,* 41–45.

Harste, J., Woodward, V., & Burke, C. (1984). *Language stories and literacy lessons.* Portsmouth, NH: Heinemann.

Harste, J., Short, K., & Burke, C. (1988). *Creating classrooms for authors.* Portsmouth, NH: Heinemann.

Harste, J. & Vasquez, V. (1998). The work we do: Journal as audit trail. *Language Arts, 75* (4), 266–276.

Leland, C., & Harste, J. (1994). Multiple ways of knowing: Curriculum in a new key. *Language Arts, 71,* 337–345.

Levi, R. (1991). *Art and music as composing processes.* Unpublished doctoral dissertation, Wayne State University, Detroit.

Martens, P. (1996). *I already know how to read.* Portsmouth, NH: Heinemann.

Short, K. (1990, December). *Learning: Making connections across sign systems.* Paper presented at the National Reading Conference, Miami Beach, FL.

Short, K., Harste, J., & Burke, C. (1996). *Creating classrooms for authors and inquirers* (2nd ed.). Portsmouth, NH: Heinemann.

Short, K., Schroeder, J., Laird, J., Kauffman, G., Ferguson, M., & Crawford, K. (1996). *Learning together through inquiry: From Columbus to integrated curriculum.* York, ME: Stenhouse.

Siegel, M. (1984). *Reading as signification.* Unpublished doctoral dissertation, Indiana University at Bloomington.

Siegel, M. (1995). More than words: The generative power of transmediation. *Canadian Journal of Education, 20* (4), 455–475.

Stephens, D. (1994). Learning that art means. *Language Arts, 71,* 34–37.

Whitin, P. (1996). *Sketching stories, stretching minds.* Portsmouth, NH: Heinemann.

Others Campbell Hill, B. & Ruptic, C. (1994). Practical aspects of authentic assessment: Putting the pieces together. Norwood, MA: Christopher-Gordon.

Cochran-Smith, M. & Lytle, S. (1993). *Inside/Outside: Teacher research and knowledge.* New York: Teachers College Press.

Csikszentmihalyi, M. (1996, Summer). How to measure learning. *The Institute View.* Los Angeles: The Paul Getty Center for Education in the Arts.

Cunningham, D. (1992). Beyond educational psychology: Steps toward an educational semiotic. *Educational Psychology Review, 4,* 165–194.

Dixson-Krauss, L. (1996). *Vygotsky in the classroom: Mediated literacy instruction and assessment*. White Plains, NY: Longman Publishers.

Dyson, A. (1995). The courage to write: Child meaning making in a contested world. *Language Arts, 72*, 324–333.

Edwards, C., Gandini, L., & Forman, G. (Eds.). (1993). *The hundred languages of children: The Reggio Emilia approach to early childhood*. Norwood, NJ: Ablex.

Eisner, E. W. (1982). *Cognition and curriculum*. New York: Longman.

Ericksen, F. (1985). Qualitative research on teaching. In M.Wittrock (Ed.) *Handbook on research on teaching* (3rd ed.). New York: Macmillan.

Forman, G. & Gandini, L. (1994). *An amusement park for the birds*. [Video]. Amherst, MA: Performanetics.

Gallas, K. (1994). *The languages of learning: How children talk, write, dance, draw, and sing their understanding of the world*. New York: Teachers College Press.

Gardner, Howard. (1983). *Frames of mind: The theory of multiple intelligences*. New York: Heinemann.

Getty Center for Education in the Arts (1993). Discipline-based art education and cultural diversity. *Crossing the boundaries*, Los Angeles, CA: The Paul Getty Center for Education in the Arts, 3–5.

Heath, S. B. (1996). The sense of being literate. *Handbook of reading research*. Mahwah, NJ: Lawrence Erlbaum Associates, Inc.

Holoquist, M. (1990). *Dialogism: Bakhtin and his world*. New York: Routledge.

Hubbard, R. (1989). *Authors of pictures, draughtsmen of words*. Portsmouth, NH: Heinemann.

Hubbard, R. & Power, B. (1993). *The art of classroom inquiry: A handbook for teacher researchers*. Portsmouth, NH: Heinemann.

John-Steiner, V. (1985). *Notebooks of the mind: Explorations of thinking*. Albuquerque: University of New Mexico Press.

Krashen, S. (1985). *The input hypothesis: Issues and implications*. New York: Longman.

Ladson-Billings, G. (1996, December 6). *The call of "whose" stories: Understanding the literacy practices of successful teachers of African American students*. Paper presented at the National Reading Conference, Charleston, SC.

Luke, A. (1995). When basic skills and information processing just aren't enough: Rethinking reading in new times, *Teachers College Record*, *97* (1), 95–115.

Meier, D. (1995*). The power of their ideas: Lessons for America from a small school in Harlem*. Boston: Beacon Press.

Myers, M. (1996). *Changing our minds*. Urbana, IL: National Council of Teachers of English.

Newkirk, T. (1989). *More than stories: The range of children's writing*. Portsmouth, NH: Heinemann.

Schubert, W. & Ayres, W. (1992). *Teacher lore: Learning from our own experiences*. White Plains, NY: Longman.

Shor, I. (1990). Liberation education: An interview with Ira Shor, *Language Arts*, *67*, 342–353.

Simon, R. (1992). *Teaching against the grain: Texts for a pedagogy of possibility*. New York: Bergin & Garvey.

Solomon, J. (1988). *Signs of our times*. Los Angeles: Jeremy Tarcher, Inc.

Suhor, C. (1992). Semiotics and the English language arts. *Language Arts*, *69*, 228–230.

Sumara, D. (1996). A life that includes reading: Understanding reading as embodied action. In D. Leu, C. Kinzer, and K. Hinchman (Eds.), *Literacies for the 21st century: Research and practice*. Chicago, IL: National Reading Conference.

Vygotsky, L. (1978). *Mind and society: The development of higher psychological processes*. In M. Cole, V. John-Steiner, S. Scribner, and E. Souberman (Eds.). Cambridge: Harvard University Press.

Wells, G. (1994). Text, talk, and inquiry: Schooling as semiotic apprenticeship. In N. Brad (Ed.), *Language and learning*. Hong Kong: Institute of Language Education.

Wolk, S. (1998). *A democratic classroom*. Portsmouth, NH: Heinemann.

Children's Books

Bunting, E. (1991). *Fly away home*. Boston: Houghton Mifflin.

DePaola, T. (1996). *The legend of blue bonnet*. New York: Putnam Publishers.

Hutchins, P. (1968). *Rosie's walk*. New York: Greenwillow.

Jonas, A. (1984). *The quilt*. New York: Greenwillow.

Ryder, J. (1982). *Snail's spell*. New York: Scholastic.

Scieszka, J. (1989). *The true story of the three little pigs*. Illus. L. S. Smith. New York: Scholastic.

Sendak, M. (1962). *Chicken soup with rice*. New York: Harper & Row.

Authors

Beth Berghoff is assistant professor of education at Indiana University at Purdue, where she coordinates the curriculum for and teaches literacy classes to a cohort of elementary education majors at Cold Spring School, an urban Professional Development School. Dr. Berghoff has been interested in inquiry and multiple ways of knowing ever since she taught in an urban 4/5/6 multiage classroom and observed how differently the students learned. She completed her dissertation research on curriculum based on inquiry and multiple ways of knowing in Susan Hamilton's first grade, and, most recently, she has been collaborating with other professors to create this type of curriculum for her undergraduate students.

Kathryn A. Egawa is currently serving as associate executive director at the National Council of Teachers of English, supporting the efforts of the elementary and middle-level membership of the Council and leading NCTE's national professional development project, The Reading Initiative. Dr. Egawa has spent the last twenty-two years in primary classrooms, three years of which included a position as an elementary librarian. She and her colleagues continue their inquiries into alternative assessment, the practical applications of literacy theory, and professional development that builds from classroom contexts. She acknowledges that the kind of inquiry she and Barry achieved could not have taken place without the support of capable public school leadership, in this case, principal Jeff Newport of the Lake Washington School District, Redmond, Washington.

Jerome C. Harste is distinguished professor of education at Indiana University where he holds the Armstrong Chair in Teacher Education. Together with a group of teachers in Indianapolis, Dr. Harste began the Center for Inquiry, a public, urban elementary school that features inquiry-based education and curriculum that supports multiple ways of knowing. Dr. Harste's interest in multiple ways of knowing began when he and his colleagues were conducting research on what young children knew about reading and writing before entering school, a project that won them NCTE's David H. Russell Research Award for Outstanding Contributions to the Teaching of English. Professor Harste is currently Vice President of NCTE.

Barry T. Hoonan believes teaching is much like poetry. It is crafted, it is magical and powerful when shared, and, in the act, it illuminates the tiny details of living and learning. For sixteen years, Barry has enjoyed teaching and learning beside students ages six to thirteen. He has twice taught in Great Britain on the Fulbright Teacher Exchange. Barry is currently teaching on Bainbridge Island, Washington, in a multiage program, grades four to six. He serves as a consultant to school districts conducting poetry, writing, and arts integration workshops. Barry's insights and notions of learning continue to expand as he watches his seven-year-old daughter, Isabelle, pen her whimsical drawings, and his three-year-old son, Keats, dance to anything with a decent beat.

This book was typeset in Avant Garde and Palatino by Electronic Imaging.
Typefaces used on the cover and spine were Usherwood Book, Eras Medium, and Paisley.
This book was printed on Lynx Opaque, 60-lb. paper, by Versa Press, Inc.